The *Motivated* Networker

*A Proven System to Leverage Your Network
in a Job Search*

Brian E. Howard, JD, CCMC, CJSS
Certified Career Management Coach
Certified Job Search Strategist

Published in the United States by WriteLife Publishing, Inc.
www.writelife.com

978-1-60808-158-5 (p)
978-1-60808-159-2 (e)

Library of Congress Control Number: 2016942431
Book design by Robin Krauss, www.bookformatters.com
Cover design by Ellis Dixon, ellisdixon.com

Other Books in The Motivated Series

The Motivated Job Search
Over 50 and Motivated
The Motivated Job Search Workbook
Motivated Resumes

To my parents, Gene and Phyllis Howard, who instilled in me at a young age the value of a strong work ethic, perseverance, and a desire to achieve.

To my father, who intuitively knew how to professionally and successfully network before the term "networking" was coined. He followed the golden rule of networking—treat others as you would want to be treated.

Message from the Author

The importance of a professional network in today's job market cannot be overstated. Having relationships and being connected to other professionally relevant people is arguably one of the most valuable assets you have for a job search. These relationships and people will support you emotionally in your job search, advise you, connect and direct you, and help you tap into the Hidden Job Market. They can lead you to your next job!

Over the course of my career as an executive recruiter, I have seen well-qualified individuals struggle when it comes to professionally networking for a job. Some allow their pride to get in the way, others don't want to come across as pushy or needy, while others are simply unorganized in what they are doing. They have the best of intentions, but all too often their efforts fail to meet their job search expectations.

I wrote this book to put focus on and form to a job seeker's networking efforts. Motivation and effort are important, but effective networking is more than just "getting out there." It must be approached with understanding, a strategic plan, and true knowledge of what it means to engage in professional networking.

A robust network and refined networking skills will serve you well in a job search and throughout your entire professional life. The positive effects on your job search and your career from nurturing professional relationships are astounding!

This book is the culmination of a career's worth of advice, frontline experience, and research on the topic of professional networking during a job search. It is written for you as a helping hand so you can more effectively use the most valuable tool you have in your job search—your professional network!

—Brian E. Howard

The Twelve Most Important Principles and Tools for Successful Job Search Networking

1. **Embrace a networking mentality**—Concentrate on building relationships for the long term. Be sincere. Be helpful. Be present in the moment. Listen and learn.

2. **Prepare an elevator speech**—Focus on an accomplishment(s) to create differentiation.

3. **Create the appropriate business card**—Emphasize key accomplishments and branding.

4. **Identify "high value" professionals who can help you or hire you**—These are professionals who can move your job search forward.

5. **Connect with "high value" professionals**—Reach out to these professionals using various means, including LinkedIn, email, calls, and so on.

6. **Engage with "high value" professionals**—When communicating, focus on the conversation, be interested, listen, and learn.

7. **Prepare and plan**—Do your research on people and their companies before a networking opportunity. Plan, prioritize, and strategize for the best use of your time.

8. **Always offer to help**—This goes straight to the heart of professional networking. Offer to help others and they will try to return the favor. Give to receive.

9. **Always follow up and follow through**—Follow up after every networking engagement and especially follow through on any action items you promised.

10. **Stay in touch**—Do not be a hit-and-run networker. Have the appropriate level of communication consistent with the level of the relationship (current or desired). "Drip market" yourself at appropriate frequency.

11. **Evaluate and improve**—Occasionally reflect upon all facets of your networking efforts. Look for areas that need improvement.

12. **Have a complete LinkedIn profile**—This allows your networking contacts to get a complete picture of who you are. Your profile must align exactly with your elevator speech, resume, business card, or any other messaging.

All of these topics and more are thoroughly discussed in the pages that follow.

Table of Contents

PART I

The Necessary Preparations for Networking

Don't bunt. Aim out of the ballpark.
Aim for the company of immortals.
— David Ogilvy[1]

This networking book is written for career-minded professionals who want to leverage their professional network and improve their networking skills to enhance their job search.

The approach is simple: Each topic is designed to tell you what you need to know and what you need to do to successfully use networking to get a job. Every effort was taken to write this book in straightforward language, assuming that the reader already has

---

1 "David Ogilvy Quotable Quote," Goodreads, http://www.goodreads.com/quotes/262108-don-t-bunt-aim-out-of-the-ballpark-aim-for-the (accessed May 28, 2015).

a basic understanding of networking and hiring practices in the business world.

Using Psychology When Networking

It's beneficial to talk briefly about the psychology of persuasion and how it will affect your networking conversations (and your overall job search).

What follows are some very important concepts that can benefit you in your networking efforts. Knowing them will help you maximize your success.

According to Robert Cialdini, a leader in the field of psychology and persuasion, there are six principles that persuade others to think and act as they do. They are:

1. Scarcity
2. Authority
3. Liking
4. Social Proof
5. Consistency and Commitment
6. Reciprocity/Reciprocation[2]

We will briefly discuss these principles and how they relate to your networking.

Scarcity

If a job seeker is viewed to be unique, special, or scarce, he or she is seen as valuable.[3] How do you capitalize upon the persuasion principle of scarcity? Answer: Differentiation.

Creating differentiation (separation) between you and other job seekers is important when you network. During the course of

---

2   Cialdini, Robert B. *Influence: Science and Practice*, 4th ed. (Needham Heights, MA: Allyn & Bacon, 2001), quoted in Kurtzberg and Naquin, *Essentials*, chapter 5, p. 94–101.

3   Cialdini, *Influence*, p. 204–205, quoted in Kurtzberg and Naquin, Essentials, p. 94–101.

conversations and communications, seemingly small and isolated thoughts of differentiation—such as he/she dresses well, is knowledgeable on industry trends, has a professional designation, and so on—compound upon themselves in the minds of those you interact with. All of this affects your perceived value and motivates people to continue the engagement with you. The more uniquely you can justifiably portray yourself while networking, the more you are using the persuasion principle of scarcity.

Authority

Most people respond to and respect authority, whether it is a title, position, professional designation, or station in life.[4] A good example of creating intangible authority is appropriate attire: A starched white shirt or stylish blouse, pressed suit, polished hard-soled shoes, the pen you use, or even the watch you wear can all convey authority that others may react to favorably. Any networking technique or information that triggers professional respect (or elevation) is using the persuasion principle of authority.

Liking

Sixty percent of most hires are based on personal chemistry (between the hiring executive and the job seeker).[5] In other words, hiring executives are persuaded to hire job seekers they personally like. This concept is equally applicable to networking. People want to interact and help others they like or with whom they have a common bond. Getting others to like you is often based on similarity or common interests. We tend to like people similar to ourselves.[6]

---

4 Cialdini, *Influence*, p. 180–185, quoted in Kurtzberg and Naquin, Essentials, p. 94–101.

5 Diane DiResta, interview by Christina Canters, "Episode 29—How to Blitz Your Job Interview—Secrets of Executive Speech Coach Diane DiResta," *DesignDrawSpeak*, podcast audio, June 12, 2014, http://designdrawspeak.com/029/ (accessed June 19, 2015).

6 Byrne, Donn Erwin. *The Attraction Paradigm*. (New York: Academic Press, 1971), quoted in Kurtzberg and Naquin, *Essentials*, p. 35.

When networking with new people, there are several ways to lay the foundation for similarity and personal chemistry. Here are a few ideas:

1. Mentioning common industry associations or groups

2. Discussing common personal interests

3. Acknowledging common former employers

4. Giving the hiring executive a sincere compliment

5. Name dropping (identifying common friends or professional colleagues)

6. Being employed (perhaps formerly employed) by an industry-leading or innovative company

Using any networking technique that creates a positive impression based on association or personal chemistry relies on the persuasion principle of liking.

Social Proof

What others say about you is more persuasive than what you say about yourself. That's the power of social proof.

Networking relies heavily on social proof, especially when it comes to being introduced or recommended by someone the contact knows. This common connection opens the door to a productive engagement. It breaks the ice and starts the conversation from an initial positive first impression.

Any networking technique that uses an introduction, recommendation, or positive affirmation as the basis for the contact is using the persuasion principle of social proof.

Consistency and Commitment

People desire a reputation of upholding their own commitments and generally do not like to go back on their word.[7] It's that simple.

One example of this principle in action is when you close a networking conversation and the contact indicates the he or she will do something for you. It will be more difficult to retreat from that course of action due to the persuasion principle of consistency and commitment.

Any networking technique that creates a self-imposed course of action (from the perspective of a networking contact) is using the persuasion principle of consistency and commitment.

Reciprocity

There is a strong psychological motivation to return favors and not to feel indebted to others. People feel compelled to repay others. This can be especially true if the item (of whatever nature) was given for free.[8]

An example of using this persuasion technique in networking would be providing a free sales lead, nonproprietary industry information, or information about the whereabouts of a colleague. To be most effective, the gesture should be made with the expectation of receiving nothing in return, but with the awareness that the psychology of reciprocity is present.

Any networking technique that endears you to a contact by doing something for him or her (especially for free) is using the persuasion principle of reciprocity. (For an example of reciprocity, see the Referring and Connecting topic later in this book.)

By raising your awareness of these persuasion principles, you will be on the alert for opportunities, and be able to capitalize upon

---

7 Cialdini, *Influence*, p. 53, quoted in Kurtzberg and Naquin, Essentials, p. 94–101.

8 Cialdini, *Influence*, p. 144, 161, quoted in Kurtzberg and Naquin, Essentials, p. 94–101.

them when they present themselves. You can use the psychology and persuasion principles to advance your networking efforts.

Now that you have a basic understanding of the principles of persuasion, you understand the reasons for (and persuasive power of) some of the networking techniques presented throughout this book—the same techniques used by many others, to their success. As you go along, try to identify the persuasion principle (there could be more than one) that makes a technique useful. Occasional reference is made to these persuasion principles to help you be more effective.

Answering Questions about Your Unemployment – Your Exit Statement

As you network, and should you be unemployed, it is inevitable that you will be asked questions like: What happened? Why are you looking for a job? Why are you unemployed? These kinds of questions can create an awkward moment unless you are prepared with a professional, honest response. That response needs to be fit for social gatherings, networking with colleagues and potential employers, and be fair to your former employer. Write your explanation and commit it to memory. Remember these concepts to help you formulate your response about your unemployment:

1. **Keep it aligned.** Make sure your statement reflects what happened and what your former employer may say.

2. **Keep it positive.** Do not make any negative statements about your former company, boss, and colleagues.

3. **Keep it factual.** Do not load emotions into your explanation.

4. **Keep it short.** Do not get into an extended explanation. Make your statement and be done.

Some poor explanations would be:

• "Those jerks over at XYZ can't find their butts with both hands! Yet they fired me!"

- "I gave XYZ twenty-five years of my life and what did it get me? A ticket in the unemployment line, that's what!"

Here are some good, brief explanations:

- "The company went through a reorganization."
- "The company was purchased."
- "The company had to make budget cuts and there were departmental layoffs. I was a casualty."
- "Based on company direction, we mutually agreed to part ways."

If you follow this advice, you will reduce the probability of additional probing questions regarding your circumstances.

Awareness of Your Transferable Job Skills and Professional Qualities

Start by doing what's necessary, then do what's possible, and suddenly you are doing the impossible.
— St. Francis of Assisi[9]

In preparing for networking, you need to raise your awareness of your transferrable skills and professional qualities. By knowing them you will be able to weave them into your verbal and written communications. This becomes persuasive when you add an accomplishment as proof of using a transferrable skill or professional quality. When you do, you differentiate yourself from others (persuasion principle of scarcity).

---

9 "Doing What's Necessary, What's Possible, and What Seems to be Impossible," *The Recovery Ranch*, http://www.recoveryranch.com/articles/necessary-possible-impossible/ (accessed May 27, 2015).

Transferrable job skills come in two forms. First are the technical skills (expertise or ability) of your profession.[10]

If you are an engineer, you know engineering things. An accountant has skills related to accounting, and so on. We will refer to these skills as your "hard" skills.[11]

Hard skills can be transferrable by convincing an employer that your skills can be easily repurposed and still be valuable to the employer.[12] An oversimplified example is an accountant using math skills in a new role.

The second type of transferable job skills used in most professional-level positions is "soft." They are in addition to your technical expertise. Here is a list of some sought-after soft transferrable job skills (not listed in any order of preference):

- **Communication Skills (writing, listening, and speaking)**— This is the most frequently mentioned skill employers desire.[13]

- **Analytical Ability (problem solving)**—This is your ability to view a situation, identify issues, evaluate relevant information, and implement a plan.[14]

- **Time Management (prioritizing)**—This is your ability to prioritize and devote the appropriate amount of time to a task.[15]

- **Innovation (out-of-the-box thinking)**—This involves harnessing creativity, reasoning skill, and what you've learned in life to solve problems.

---

10 Yate, Martin John. Knock 'em Dead—*The Ultimate Job Search Guide*. Avon, MA: Adams Media, 2014. p. 19.

11 Ibid., p. 32.

12 Leanne, Shelly. *How to Interview Like a Top MBA: Job-Winning Strategies from Headhunters, Fortune 100 Recruiters, and Career Counselors*. (New York: McGraw-Hill, 2004), p. 104.

13 Hansen, Randall S., PhD, and Katharine Hansen, PhD. "What Do Employers Really Want? Top Skills and Values Employers Seek from Job-Seekers," *Quintessential Careers*, http://www.quintcareers.com/job_skills_values.html (accessed May 27, 2015).

14 Yate, *Knock 'em Dead*, p. 23–24.

15 Ibid., p. 25.

- **Collaboration (teamwork)**—This means working with others toward a shared goal.[16]

- **Management (people leadership)**—This is your ability to gain buy-in or respect from a team, lead by defining goals and methods, and manage and guide a group toward shared goals or production targets.

- **Customer Focus (customer service)**—This is your understanding that your employer must please and serve customers to be successful.

- **Business Understanding (business acumen)**—This is your ability to understand the business realities and the influences in the market and how they affect your employer.[17]

Closely aligned with the concept of transferrable job skills are Professional Qualities. Here is a list of professional qualities respected by others:

- **Honesty**—This is the foundation of every relationship. A networking contact (and an employer) must be able to trust you and respect you as a professional for the relationship to last and flourish.[18]

- **Positive Attitude**—Make no mistake—this is a big deal. Others are attracted to people who show enthusiasm, energy, and a positive outlook.[19] Displaying a positive attitude gives you a competitive advantage when networking.

- **Interpersonal Relationships**—Employers want employees

16 Ibid., and Hansen and Hansen, "What Do Employers *Really* Want?"

17 Grant Tilus, "Top 10 Human Resources Job Skills Employers Want to See," (blog), *Rasmussen College*, July 29, 2013, http://www.rasmussen.edu/degrees/business/blog/human-resources-job-skills-employers-want-to-see/ (accessed July 10, 2015).

18 Hansen and Hansen, "What Do Employers *Really* Want?"

19 Victoria Andrew, "The Power of a Positive Attitude," (blog), Kavaliro Employment Agency, May 23, 2013, http://www.kavaliro.com/the-power-of-a-positive-attitude (accessed June 8, 2015).

who can get along with other potential coworkers. They avoid those who "rock the boat" and do not fit the culture.

- **Work Ethic**—Employers seek employees who put forth their best effort at all times. They seek out employees who are motivated and internally driven. They want employees who are persistent and passionate about their jobs.[20]

- **Dependable**—Employers seek out employees who will show up on time. They want to rest assured you will "be there" for the company. If you are a remote employee, they want to trust you are working even though you are out of sight.

- **Willingness to Learn**—This is your intellectual flexibility, curiosity, and your ability not to get stuck in your own ways. Regardless of your tenure, be willing to learn about new technology and improve your skills (and discover new ones). Markets change. Business changes. Your industry changes. You must be open and pursue opportunities to learn and change.[21] Doing so increases your value and marketability as a professional. **As a professional, you never want to stop learning and growing.**

Some job seekers have difficulty identifying transferrable skills and professional qualities because they have not had to think about them for a while. They've been doing their jobs, not thinking about the skills they've been using to succeed. That's normal. There are a couple of ideas that can help you expand upon your transferrable skills (and perhaps your professional qualities). Think about your last position or two. What skills did you use? Now, think how you can break down those skills into smaller elements. For example, let's say you were in sales. What does that skill really entail? What's really going on there? Plenty!

---

20 Hansen and Hansen, "What Do Employers *Really* Want?"
21 Ibid.

- Research on target industries
- Cold calling
- Persuasive verbal skills
- Presentation skills
- Closing
- Follow up

- Identifying decision makers
- Email marketing
- Articulation of value proposition
- Overcoming objections
- Negotiating
- And so much more . . .

By identifying these skills, you can open yourself to networking opportunities and employers who are searching for job seekers with these skills.

Once you have identified your transferrable job skills and professional qualities, there are several things you can do with this valuable information. Your skills and qualities could be:

- A component of your branding message.
- Woven into the Summary section of your resume and LinkedIn profile.
- Mentioned in a Core Skills, Experience, or Accomplishments section of your resume.
- Used to write success stories.
- Used in cover letters and emails.
- Used as a part of your elevator speech.
- Used in networking conversations.
- Used in interviews.[22]
- And so on . . .

The key to using these skills in your networking efforts is to promote those skills and your unique professional qualities as valuable. To do that, tie in an accomplishment as evidence of the value of those skills and qualities. Provide success stories of the skills and qualities in action. (More on that in a moment.) Providing this connection is especially persuasive while networking.

---

22 Yate, *Knock 'em Dead*, p. 30.

Branding

Always remember: a brand is the most valuable piece of
real estate in the world; a corner of someone's mind.
— John Hegarty[23]

As a job seeker, it is imperative that you craft a professional brand that announces to the marketplace your distinct talents and what you represent. The process of branding is discovering who you are, what you are, your unique abilities, and communicating them through various mediums to your network or target market. To help you in crafting a brand, this section and the following one on the elevator speech work in tandem.

There are numerous benefits of creating an impactful brand, including:

1. You differentiate yourself from other job seekers, and gain a huge advantage.

2. You create the initial impression networking contacts have of you.

3. You more quickly convey your value.

4. You more easily match your skills and value proposition to a potential opening.

5. You better determine which opportunities to pursue.[24]

The drawback of not having a professional brand is simple: You become a commodity. There is no perceived differentiation of you from other job seekers. As a result, you cannot command a premium and have reduced leverage when it comes to compensation. Perhaps

---

23 "10 Ways You're Building a Fantastic Brand," *Design Aglow* (blog), February 3, 2015, http://designaglow.com/blogs/design-aglow/16728432-10-ways-youre-building-a-fantastic-brand (accessed May 28, 2015).

24 Whitcomb, *Job Search Magic*, p. 122.

worse, others will determine for themselves what they want to see in you. They will cast you in a light based on their own conclusions, which may not be the message you want to communicate.[25]

Perhaps the biggest benefit to creating a professional brand is the self-awareness of your unique skills, experience, and the internal, emotional recognition of your passions. You will project the value of your abilities more clearly, resulting in networking for jobs that are a better match to your background and experience.

The professional branding process requires introspection and thoughtful reflection. In some cases, thinking through your branding can be both an emotional and a professionally enlightening event.

Think of it this way: As a networker, you want to connect with others for "right-fit" job opportunities. Having a well-crafted, professional brand helps you achieve that. You must be perceived as the right candidate; and through branding, you are better able to align yourself to a "right-fit" job opportunity.

Keep in mind that the effectiveness of your brand is determined by the connection that exists between what the brand claims and what it can actually deliver. In other words, you must be able to prove and quantify your professional brand through accomplishments and success stories. Failing to do so will have disastrous results. Don't oversell your brand and capabilities. Doing so will lead you to positions that are not the right fit for you.

Create a succinct brand. Think of it, in analogous terms, as a tagline or a theme that will be the foundation for networking and your job search.

To help determine your brand, ask yourself some questions:

1. What am I good at or an expert in?

2. What have I been recognized for?

3. What is my reputation with others (subordinates, peers, senior management)?

---

25 Ibid.

4. What have been my strong points in past job reviews (if applicable)?

5. What differentiates me from others with the same job?

6. What professional qualities do I have that make me good at my job?

7. What are the professional achievements I am most proud of?[26]

The answers to these questions and the thoughts they provoke are essential to forming your brand. Now, synthesize the answers and thoughts into single words or short phrases that capture the concept of your responses. Here are some examples:

Sales
Consistently exceeding sales goals. Award-winning sales professional.

Operations Management
Dedicated to improved operational efficiency through effective leadership.

Account Management
Client-minded problem solver focused on client satisfaction and retention.

ERISA[27] Lawyer
Protecting ERISA fiduciaries from the Department of Labor.

A branding statement could also be a few separate descriptive words or phrases:

---

26 Ibid., Chapter 5, "Communicate Your Value Via a Career Brand."

27 "Employee Retirement Income Security Act"; see "Frequently Asked Questions About Retirement Plans and ERISA," US Department of Labor, http://www.dol.gov/ebsa/faqs/faq_consumer_pension.html (accessed July 8, 2015).

Process Improvement • *Lean Six Sigma*[28]
• *Turn-around Specialist*
Marketing • *Advertising* • *Public Relations*

Branding Is Important

Creating and deciding on a brand is important. Take the necessary time to reflect on this (which will vary from person to person). What you decide your brand is will form the foundation for much of what will follow in your job search and networking efforts.

You may discover several skills and abilities to showcase in your brand. But, for the purposes of your networking, focus on promoting your top one or two choices only. Mention other skills, which will happen naturally during networking conversations and interviews. The purpose of branding is to get you known for your value, introduced and recommended by others, and differentiate you from other job seekers.

Elevator Speech

The only people who don't need elevator pitches are elevator salesmen. — Jarod Kintz[29]

The elevator speech is a critical component to networking. By definition, an elevator speech is "the 30-second speech that summarizes who you are, what you do, and why you'd be a perfect candidate."[30] In essence, it is your personal commercial.

---

28 A process that resolves problems while reducing costs; see "What is Lean Six Sigma?" Go Lean Six Sigma, https://goleansixsigma.com/what-is-lean-six-sigma/ (accessed July 8, 2015).

29 "Jarod Kintz Quotable Quote," Goodreads, http://www.goodreads.com/quotes/1234580-the-only-people-who-don-t-need-elevator-pitches-are-elevator (accessed May 28, 2015).

30 Collamer, Nancy. "The Perfect Elevator Pitch To Land A Job," *Forbes*, February 4, 2013, http://www.forbes.com/sites/nextavenue/2013/02/04/the-perfect-elevator-pitch-to-land-a-job/ (accessed May 28, 2015).

The purpose of your elevator speech is to grab the listener's attention, quickly provide relevant information, and initiate conversation. A crisply delivered elevator speech is a differentiator. While others may struggle and stumble, you will be able to concisely inform the listener about your professional value proposition (brand).

Develop a handful of variations, depending upon the situation, including all forms of networking, association and industry conferences, and social gatherings.

Here are some tips on crafting your elevator speech (some examples are at the end of this section):

1. Know your target audience.

This single factor will give your speech the most impact. For example, if you're targeting a CEO position and you will be speaking to members of the board of directors, you want your elevator speech to include statements of vision, direction, strategy, profitability, and shareholder value (especially for publicly traded companies).

If your target position is in operations and the hiring executive is the COO, you want your elevator speech to contain concepts such as efficiency and operational savings.

Finally, if your target position is in sales and the hiring executive will be the director or vice president of sales, you want your elevator speech to contain information about new business sales and sales goal attainment.

2. Know what your value proposition is.

This is where your branding comes into full play. Identify as precisely as possible what you offer, what problems you can solve, and what benefits you bring to an employer.

3. Outline your speech.

Give yourself some time to ponder the ideas and concepts you may include—it isn't necessary to start drafting the speech immediately, but begin with notes reminding you of your bottom-line message. Don't worry about proper grammar and complete sentences yet. The objective is to gather concepts and ideas first, so be careful not to edit yourself. Refer back to the concepts you used to form your brand.

4. Write your speech.

Now that you have ideas and concepts about yourself to promote, begin drafting your speech's initial version. Here is a formula to help you:

A. Identify yourself by function.

B. Include a statement regarding your value proposition as a professional (what problems you solve).

C. Mention accomplishments or proof statements that support your value proposition as a professional.

D. End with a call to action in the form of a subtle invitation to have a conversation.

5. Tailor the speech to them, not you.

Remember the people listening to you will be tuned into WIIFM (What's In It For Me?). So, refer to what you have written to ensure your message addresses their potential needs.

For example, this introduction: "I am a talent-acquisition professional with ten years of experience working for financial services companies," would be more impactful stated this way: "I am a talent-acquisition professional with a strong track record of identifying and recruiting top-level sales talent." Hear the difference?

Using terminology that focuses on the benefits you bring will get the listener's attention. Benefit-focused terminology persuades the listener that you have the skills and track record of success necessary for the job.

6. Practice, practice, practice—and solicit feedback.

Read your speech aloud. Then, tinker with the words (the goal is to have a speech that sounds authentic and confident). Now, memorize the speech and rehearse it. Consider practicing in front of a mirror and record it on your smartphone. Granted, this might feel awkward at first, but the more you practice, the more conversational your delivery will be. Smiling while saying the words will increase the impact of the speech. Project your voice so those listening will clearly hear and understand.

Practice your speech until it no longer sounds rehearsed. When you are ready, try the speech out on some of your friends. Make eye contact, smile, and deliver your message with confidence. Afterward, ask them what they think. If their response doesn't line up with what you want from your speech, the speech still needs work.

7. Prepare a few variations.

You will naturally want to say things differently to a colleague than you would to a personal friend at a social gathering. Sometimes you'll have just fifteen seconds for your speech, and in other situations you might have a full minute.

Focus on your key talking points, and then create ways to customize your speech for different situations. Much of this will happen naturally as you speak with people (as long as you remember your talking points).

The word-count feature on your computer can help you create shorter and longer versions. A good rule of thumb is that you can comfortably say about 150 words in sixty seconds.[31]

Remember, the purpose of an elevator speech is to quickly inform the listener of your value proposition as a professional and begin a conversation. Putting these tips into action is the real trick. Check out these websites that contain scores of elevator speeches (not all

are designed for job seekers) for a variety of industries: http://www.improvandy.com and http://www.yourelevatorpitch.net.

---

31 Walters, Lillet. *Secrets of Successful Speakers: How You Can Motivate, Captivate, and Persuade.* New York: McGraw-Hill, 1993, p. 59.

Examples

Employee Benefits Sales Professional

"I am an employee benefits sales professional who helps businesses control their healthcare and insurance costs. My expertise is in medical self-funding and population health management. I have a documented track record of exceeding sales goals; in fact, over the last five years I have exceeded goals by an average of twenty-one percent. I want to make a career move to an organization looking to expand its market share in the self-funded arena."

Sales Management Executive: Focus on mentorship

"I am a sales management executive, and my forte is training and mentoring sales professionals to achieve higher sales production. During my twenty-year career, I have turned around underperforming sales professionals and trained and mentored several award-winning sales reps. On average, over the course of my career, my sales teams have met or exceeded their group production goals more than eighty-five percent of the time. I'm looking to make a career move to an organization that needs sales leadership to grow sales and market share."

Operations Professional: Focus on efficiency

"I am an operations professional, and I specialize in improving efficiencies and expense reduction. In fact, during my last position I decreased customer response time by more than sixty-five percent and reduced departmental expenses by eighteen percent by realigning personnel to positions that better fit their skills. I want to make a career move to an organization that desires to save money by making operations more efficient."

Accounting: Focus on cost savings

"I am a CPA who specializes in identifying cost-saving opportunities in manufacturing. With my former employer, I saved more than $750,000 over five years by negotiating return credits with vendors, increasing cash flow through accounts receivable, and decreasing collections. I want to make a job change to a manufacturing organization that can benefit from my abilities to identify cost-saving opportunities."

Elevator speeches can emphasize different value propositions. If you discover a particular skill is in demand with a prospective employer and you have it, change your speech to focus on that skill.

Success Stories

There is no passion to be found playing small—in settling for a life that is less than the one you are capable of living.
— Nelson Mandela[32]

A success story is a description of a career-related event that provides evidence regarding your skills, abilities, competencies, and motivation to succeed in a position or role. They can be very persuasive during networking communications. In a business context, success stories are your case studies supporting your professional value proposition.

Creating success stories is often a walk down your professional memory lane. Think about projects, challenges, and problems you have dealt with over your career, or even during a normal work week. Think in terms of identifying, preventing, and solving a problem. How did you do it? What was the positive result of your success story?[33]

It's highly recommended to compose several success stories. By writing them down and reviewing them, you will be able to more easily remember them in networking conversations. You will also

---

32 Nsehe, Mfonobong. "19 Inspirational Quotes From Nelson Mandela," Forbes.com, December 6, 2013, http://www.forbes.com/sites/mfonobongnsehe/2013/12/06/20-inspirational-quotes-from-nelson-mandela/ (accessed May 27, 2015).

33 Whitcomb, Job Search Magic, p. 119.

be able to use them in written communication and interviews.[34] These success stories will support your brand and qualifications.

Creating success stories is an easy and fun exercise in self-discovery. There is a simple formula that seems to work well for most job seekers:

C. Challenge (Situation, Task)
A. Action
R. Result[35]

Describe the challenge you faced or task you were assigned. Describe the plan of action you took and the positive result. Try to quantify the results with numbers or percentages whenever possible. A positive recommendation from a supervisor can also work well.

When you write your success stories, do so with different skills and competencies in mind (transferrable job skills and professional qualities). For example: stories that reflect true technical ability, analytical thinking, communication skills, leadership, and so on, including complementary combinations of skills and competencies within a single story.

Having success stories prewritten, rehearsed, and at your disposal will help impress networking contacts, differentiate you from other job seekers (using the persuasion principle of scarcity), and give you a competitive advantage. You will be viewed as prepared as opposed to those who choose to wing it.[36]

The Appendix in this book has a Success Story Worksheet and samples of success stories.

34 Ibid., p. 391–402, Chapter 15, "Score Points in Behavioral Interviews."

35 Safani, Barbara. "Tell a Story Interviewers Can't Forget," *TheLadders*, http://www.theladders.com/career-advice/tell-story-interviewers-cant-forget (accessed May 29, 2015).

36 Whitcomb, *Job Search Magic*, p. 119.

Business Cards

High expectations are the key to everything.
— Sam Walton[37]

Business cards are a necessity for networking. Getting a business card should be toward the top of your job search to-do list.

There are four different approaches to the standard three-and-a-half-inch by two-inch business card: traditional business cards, networking business cards, resume business cards, and infographic business cards.

To determine the best business card approach for your needs, consider this key factor: Which would be best received by a networking contact or a hiring executive for your level of position?

A solid case can be made for getting two sets of cards to use in different settings: traditional for truly social events, and a networking or resume card for job networking events.

Here are examples for each kind of job search business card:

Traditional Business Cards

This business card is simple in design. It contains only your name, city of residence, (street address is optional), telephone number(s), email address, and LinkedIn profile address. It is used for information exchange purposes only.

---

37 Bergdahl, Michael. *What I Learned From Sam Walton: How to Compete and Thrive in a Wal-Mart World.* (Hoboken, New Jersey: John Wiley & Sons, 2004), p. 39.

Bob Johnson, CSFS®

1340 Main Street	(816) 987-6543 (C)
Blue Springs, MO 64015	Bob.johnson1340@gmail.com
(816) 123-4567 (H)	www.linkedin.com/in/bobjohnson

Networking Business Cards

Networking business cards contain the same key contact information as a traditional card, except this variety also has a title and a concise statement regarding your career focus and unique value proposition or brand. Remember to keep the messaging consistent among your networking card, your elevator speech, your LinkedIn profile, your resume, and so on. With some variations, the theme of these job-seeking tools must align.

Award-Winning, Population Health Management
Sales Professional

Bob Johnson, CSFS®

National Sales Executive

1340 Main Street	(816) 987-6543 (C)
Blue Springs, MO 64015	Bob.johnson1340@gmail.com
(816) 123-4567 (H)	www.linkedin.com/in/bobjohnson

Resume Business Cards

A resume business card takes the networking card one step further. Here you may expand descriptive information on the front of the card and put key qualifications and accomplishments on the back. Don't focus on job titles or duties; instead, spotlight your top two or three accomplishments (or qualifications).

This next point is optional, but leave a little white space at the bottom of the back of the card, allowing the recipient room to jot a note about you. Hopefully the note will read, "Need to call."

Bob Johnson, CSFS®

National Sales Executive

Award-winning, population health management
sales professional with 5+ years of consistent
goal achievement

1340 Main Street	(999) 473-5678 (C)
Blue Springs, MO 64015	bob.johnson1340@gmail.com
(999) 473-1234 (H)	www.linkedin.com/in/bobjohnson

Front

Qualifications Summary

- #1 Sales Producer last three years
- Presidents Club Qualifier 2009 to present
- Consistently produced over $4M annually

Back

It's fine to mix and match the concepts of the three forms of business cards. For example, you may determine that it would be best received by your target audience that the front of the card has a traditional look. But on the back, you may choose to put a branding statement and a couple of achievements. That's fine. Exercise your best business judgment.

Business cards can be printed at most office supply stores and are reasonably inexpensive for a few hundred cards (generally under $200). In addition, many online companies produce business cards inexpensively. And if you're technology savvy, you can print your cards using special paper and a template that is already loaded on most computers.

When creating your job-search business cards, keep the design simple. Use traditional fonts and conservative, business-appropriate color schemes. If you are pursuing jobs in advertising, media marketing, or other creative fields, you have more latitude with design and use of colors.

QR Codes

A tool to consider using on your business cards (or resume) is a QR code. These static-like barcodes are found on many contemporary advertisements. QR codes have gained popularity because they can be scanned by a smartphone, which can instantly take the barcode data and connect it to contact information or a website link.

The QR code is an innovative way to differentiate you and illustrate your technology awareness. Your code can link to almost anything on the web, such as your LinkedIn profile, a thirty- to sixty-second video presentation of yourself, your personal website, blog, and so on.

Most websites used to generate QR codes are free. You can also sign up and pay a fee to track how many times your QR code has been scanned. Some QR code websites include:

www.goqr.me
http://qrcode.kaywa.com/
http://www.scanlife.com

It is really a personal judgment call as to whether a QR code should appear on the front or the back of the card. The key consideration is appearance. Be comfortable with how the card presents itself to potential employers.

Here is an example of a business card with a QR code:

Infographic Business Card

An infographic business card is a very unique concept. It is not a "business card" in the traditional sense. Instead, it is more of a "networking handbill." In concept, an infographic business card is a colorful, high-resolution document containing impactful and persuasive background information and accomplishments presented through creatively designed pie charts and bar graphs.

Conceptually, an infographic business card is larger than the standard three-and-a-half-inch by two-inch business card. Although there is no hard-and-fast rule, a four-by-six-inch card is a good starting point.

The infographic business card is ideal for networking events, especially for association gatherings and conventions. Printed on business-card-grade paper, with colorful graphics, it is a clear differentiator. If not too large, it can still easily slip into the inside jacket pocket or portfolio of a networking contact or hiring executive.

If this infographic card idea appeals to you, it is highly

recommended that you use the services of a professional with experience creating infographic resumes, as this experience translates well to infographic cards. You can check out Piktochart (www.piktochart.com) if you want to try-your-hand in creating your own infographic document.

Remember, business cards, regardless of whether they are networking cards, resume cards, or infographic cards are marketing pieces. Always have these cards handy, regardless of which version or versions you decide to use. You never know who you might meet who will be a good networking contact.

LinkedIn

Active participation on LinkedIn is the best way to say,
'Look at me!' without saying 'Look at me!'
— Bobby Darnell[38]

Having a complete LinkedIn profile is imperative to your networking efforts. As you network with others, they will look you up on LinkedIn. Just as important, HR recruiters and actual hiring executives search LinkedIn for qualified candidates for their open positions. This section is written with both scenarios in mind.

LinkedIn is clearly the most used and effective professional networking website on the planet, with more than 400 million members in two hundred countries.[39] In the United States alone there are more than 100 million members. At present, LinkedIn adds "more

---

38 Knyszweski, Jerome. "How to Use LinkedIn as a Student—And Nail That Dream Job," LinkedIn Pulse, April 28, 2015, https://www.linkedin.com/pulse/how-use-linkedin-student-nail-dream-job-jerome-knyszewski (accessed May 28, 2015).

39 Smith, Craig. "By the Numbers: 125+ Amazing LinkedIn Statistics." Last updated November 4, 2015, http://expandedramblings.com/index.php/by-the-numbers-a-few-important-linkedin-stats/ (accessed November 11, 2015).

than two new members every second."[40] "Over 25 million profiles are viewed on LinkedIn daily."[41]

There is a direct correlation between a complete profile (its strength) and your discoverability through LinkedIn.

LinkedIn has five levels of profile strengths:
1. Just beginning
2. Intermediate
3. Advanced
4. Expert
5. All-Star

If your profile is incomplete, it will not be impressive to a networking contact and won't register as high in searches as those that are more robust.[42] "Users with complete profiles are forty times more likely to receive opportunities through LinkedIn."[43]

What makes your profile complete?
- Your industry and location
- An up-to-date, current position (with a description)
- Two past positions
- Your education
- Your skills (minimum of 3)
- A profile photo
- At least 50 connections[44]

---

40 "About LinkedIn," *LinkedIn Newsroom,* https://press.linkedin.com/about-linkedin (accessed May 29, 2015).

41 Geoff, "Top LinkedIn Facts and Stats [Infographic]," (blog), *We Are Social Media,* July 25, 2014, http://wersm.com/top-linkedin-facts-and-stats-infographic/ (accessed May 29, 2015).

42 Reynolds, Marci. "How to Be Found More Easily in LinkedIn (LinkedIn SEO)," *Job-Hunt. org,* http://www.job-hunt.org/social-networking/be-found-on-linkedin.shtml (accessed June 4, 2015).

43 "Profile Completeness," LinkedIn, https://www.linkedin.com/static?key=pop%2Fpop_more_profile_completeness (accessed May 29, 2015).

44 Ibid.

It cannot be overemphasized. LinkedIn should be your primary online professional networking tool.

LinkedIn makes it easy to network, connect with colleagues in your industry, stay informed on industry issues and trends, research companies, and be alerted about job opportunities.

It is recommended that before you create or update a profile, you take some time and review what other professionals similar to you have done with their profiles. Take the best and incorporate the ideas into your profile.

On LinkedIn, you have complete control of your professional image and how you want to be portrayed. Here are some of the important sections and topics that create an impactful LinkedIn profile:

1. Photo

Your photo is important. It shows that you are a real person. Since LinkedIn is a professional networking site—and you are networking for a job—it is recommended to have a professional photo or, at minimum, a close-up photograph of you professionally dressed. According to experts, "profiles with a photo are fourteen times more likely to be viewed."[45]

2. Name

Use the name you commonly go by. If your given name is Richard, but you go by Rich, use Rich. It is permissible to put both your given name and the name you use in quotation marks or in parentheses.

Professional designations. There is a difference of opinion among

45 Smith, Jacquelyn. "The Complete Guide To Crafting A Perfect LinkedIn Profile," *Business Insider*, January 21, 2015, http://www.businessinsider.com/guide-to-perfect-linkedin-profile-2015-1 (accessed June 4, 2015).

commentators on this topic.[46] However, it can be to your advantage to put one or two notable professional designations behind your name. Designations should be significant to your industry, add to your credibility, or create a competitive advantage in the job market. Using one notable designation could increase your odds of having your profile viewed.

3. Headline

Your headline is that area just below your name. It is the first thing someone reads about you after your name. Make it impactful by describing yourself by using keywords or short phrases that best describe your function. "What do you want to be known for?"[47] Or found for? Think about your branding statement. Avoid superlatives or flamboyant adjectives in your headline (The Industry's Best Sales Representative on the Planet).

The headline ultimately attracts viewers with the intention that they continue to read your profile and be impressed with your experience, skills, and accomplishments. Having an impactful headline with keywords will increase the number of views you will receive.

A convenient formula that seems to work for many job seekers is: [Job function or title] + [A bridge phrase, e.g., "with experience in," or "with expertise in," or "specializing in"] + [reference to products, services, skills, industry, professional qualities, and so on].

For example: "Senior Sales Executive with Experience in Workers' Compensation, Pain Management, Leadership." "Product Development Professional Applying Behavioral Science to Healthcare Technology."

---

46 Isaacson, Nate. "Professional Designations Are Great But They Are Not A Part of Your Name," LinkedIn Pulse, April 14, 2014, https://www.linkedin.com/pulse/20140414223601-23236063-professional-designations-are-great-but-they-are-not-a-part-of-your-name (accessed July 16, 2015); Hanson, Arik. "Should You Put MBA Behind Your Name on Your LinkedIn Profile?" LinkedIn Pulse, May 29, 2014, https://www.linkedin.com/pulse/20140529131058-18098999-should-you-put-mba-behind-your-name-on-your-linkedin-profile (accessed July 17, 2015).

47 Whitcomb, *Job Search Magic*, p. 68.

4. Keywords

It is estimated that there are more than a billion searches annually on LinkedIn.[48] Companies and recruiters search keywords to find candidates (in addition to people who search for a particular company or person).

How does it work? When you perform a keyword search, your first-degree connections will be first. Of those first-degree results, completed profiles will be first (all the more the reason to have a completed profile). After that is second degree, then third. After that are your fellow LinkedIn Groups members (a superb reason to join groups, if you haven't), and finally by every other person on LinkedIn.[49]

Your profile's keywords should be as relevant and pertinent to your background as possible. This is where your industry's terms-of-art and certain abbreviations come into play. You can put these in a variety of places. According to LinkedIn, where these keywords appear can matter. Keywords in your headline, job title, summary, experience, interests, and skills rank the highest. Make sure you insert your keywords you want to be known for or found for in these places.[50]

5. Location Section

LinkedIn lists every significant metropolitan city in the country (more than 280 geographical location phrases at last count). Your location (or one very close) is likely to be listed.

It is important to put an accurate city location on your profile. When employers and recruiters conduct searches, they often look for profiles of individuals who live in a particular city or region. Having no location or a generic "United States" makes you almost invisible

---

48 Stephanie Frasco, "11 Tips To Help Optimize Your LinkedIn Profile For Maximum Exposure and Engagement," Convert with Content (blog), https://www.convertwithcontent.com/11-tips-optimize-linkedin-profile-maximum-exposure-engagement/ (accessed June 10, 2015).

49 Ibid.

50 Ibid.

to employers and recruiters who may need a qualified candidate located in a particular city or region.

6. Industry Specialty Section

Be accurate when choosing an industry specialty. LinkedIn lists 145 industry phrases, so choose the one that best fits you. When employers and recruiters, conduct searches, they may look for profiles from particular industries—ones from which they have made successful hires in the past.

Having an industry on your profile can get you fifteen times more profile views than those who do not list an industry.[51]

7. Contact Information

LinkedIn allows you to provide contact information. This is a good place to put your personal email address and perhaps your cell phone number. Providing this information makes it easier for networking contacts, recruiters, and others to reach you without having to go through LinkedIn.

8. Summary Section

The summary section is an area where you can write a three- to five-paragraph narrative of your background, experience, and achievements. This is a biographical description of your career, so keep the content professionally relevant and use keywords.

Consider making the first lines of your summary section very similar to your headline though expanded. This will increase the keyword count for those trying to discover you on LinkedIn.

There is a difference of opinion regarding how the remaining content of this section should be presented. Some advocate that it is an opportunity for you to write in the first person and show

---

51 "10 Tips for the Perfect LinkedIn Profile," LinkHumans, Slideshare, published July 1, 2014, http://www.slideshare.net/linkedin/10-tips-for-the-perfect-linkedin-profile (accessed November 11, 2015).

personality.[52] Others contend that it should be more in the third-person narrative. The choice is yours. However, make your decision based on how it will be best perceived by a networking contact or a potential employer hiring for your level of position.

Consider adding your email address in the summary section so people can contact you directly.

9. Job Experience

This is reasonably straightforward. Think resume. Use relevant keywords. Remember that your LinkedIn profile and your resume must match in general content and especially dates.

A comment about titles: If your job title is company-specific, include a translation or generic job title. For example, "Purchasing Agent" may be listed as "Product Specialist/Purchasing Representative" because those titles are more understandable outside the company/industry. A functional title educates a networking contact, hiring executive or recruiter of your employment role. According to LinkedIn, "add[ing] your two most recent work positions . . . can increase your profile views by twelve times."[53]

10. Volunteer Experience and Causes

Some employers look favorably upon profiles of those who volunteer or are involved in civic causes—it speaks to matching the culture of the company. In fact, according to LinkedIn, 42 percent of hiring executives view volunteer work and social causes as equal to formal work experience.[54]

---

52 Smith, Jacquelyn. "Here's What To Say In Your LinkedIn 'Summary' Statement," *Business Insider*, December 19, 2014, http://www.businessinsider.com/what-to-say-in-your-linkedin-summary-statement-2014-12 (accessed July 9, 2015).

53 Daniel Ayele, "Land Your Dream Job in 2015 with These Data-Proven LinkedIn Tips," LinkedIn Blog, January 29, 2015, http://blog.linkedin.com/2015/01/29/jobseeking-tips/ (accessed June 9, 2015).

54 Dougherty, Lisa. "16 Tips to Optimize Your LinkedIn Profile and Your Personal Brand," LinkedIn Pulse, July 8, 2014, https://www.linkedin.com/pulse/20140708162049-7239647-16-tips-to-optimize-your-linkedin-profile-and-enhance-your-personal-brand (accessed November 11, 2015).

11. Certifications

Listing certifications can enhance your value as a viable candidate for a position. Frequently, a professional certification or designation is a significant differentiator from other job seekers.

12. Organizations

Listing your memberships in professional associations can have an influence on networking contacts and employers because it reflects that you are in touch and following the industry. It can also be a source of networking and education.[55]

13. Skills and Endorsements

LinkedIn allows you to list fifty skills. Be reasonably specific and don't use all fifty. You don't want a potential employer to view you as a "jack of all trades and a master of none." You may appear desperate if you list too many skills. How many skills are too many? When you feel you are starting to stretch to include a skill, you have likely reached the end. According to LinkedIn, profiles with skills listed get looked at thirteen times more.[56]

Endorsements are a nice LinkedIn feature. They add credibility to your profile as others agree with the skills you have listed. People will endorse you for skills that you initially select, but they can add others. Endorsements are important because they tap into the persuasion principle of social proof.

One significant differentiating strategy is to list one or two professional qualities in your skills/endorsement section. These could include such things as honesty, integrity, and work ethic, among others. Having these qualities rank high in your endorsements section is unique and not something a networking contact, hiring executive, or recruiter sees often, which could differentiate you from others.

Endorse others. Remember, LinkedIn is a networking mechanism

---

55 Yate, *Knock 'em Dead*, p. 86.

56 Ayele, "Land Your Dream Job."

and a two-way street. The more you engage with others, the more they will engage with you.

14. Education

Start with your highest degree and work backward in reverse chronological order. If you provide dates, make sure they match your resume.

LinkedIn users "who have an education on their profile receive an average of ten times more profile views than those who don't."[57]

15. Honors and Awards

List all notable honors and awards you have received, signaling to an employer that others have recognized you for your performance. Honors and awards can create the impression of scarcity—a persuasion principle.

16. Recommendations

Remember that what others say about you can be more impactful than what you say about yourself. "Recommendations are mini testimonials that people give you who have worked with you. You can request them via LinkedIn. It's another way to build credibility [for] you and your work. Remember to return the favor when someone gives you a recommendation."[58]

Similar to endorsements, recommendations on your LinkedIn profile tap into the persuasion principle of social proof.

Many recruiters review recommendations as part of their evaluation protocols. As a minimum goal, get at least three recommendations posted on your profile from former bosses, colleagues, customers, or vendors you've interacted with.

17. Interests

This is a section where you can help improve the number of views

---

57 LinkHumans, "10 Tips."
58 Frasco, "11 Tips."

you receive compared to other job seekers. List business interests in this section using your keywords. Most job seekers don't do this. They just list personal interests. This is another place where the LinkedIn programming looks for keywords when matching what a recruiter or hiring executive is looking for in a search for candidates.

It is perfectly acceptable and encouraged to list your personal interests as well. It personalizes your profile. The point is to list both business as well as personal interests.

18. Other Areas

LinkedIn has additional sections to further customize your profile, including projects, languages, publications, test scores, courses, patents, and others. Depending upon the employer, and networking contact, these areas may impact their impression of you. You can attach images, videos, Slideshare presentations, and documents as well. These are optional and not required to get you found by an employer or recruiter. Embrace these features if you want to showcase your career experiences with examples. If you're a public speaker, consider adding a video. If you are a graphic designer, add a portfolio of your work. If you write, add an article or a chapter of your book. Consider adding anything unique or impactful to prove and reinforce your skills, experience, or achievements.

19. Keep Your Profile Current

Update your information and keep it current so it doesn't appear stale. According to LinkedIn, changing certain sections in your profile (most notably your employer), making recommendations, and following companies will be shared in the activity feed.[59] These changes can get you noticed.

---

59 "Showing or Hiding Activity Updates About You," LinkedIn Help Center, https://help.linkedin.com/app/answers/detail/a_id/78/~/showing-or-hiding-activity-updates-about-you (accessed June 2, 2015).

20. Groups

LinkedIn groups are valuable, give you a platform to be an expert in an industry or topic, and help you gain insight and knowledge. "Your profile is five times more likely to be viewed if you join and are active in groups."[60]

Networking contacts and hiring executives search LinkedIn by keywords, and they also interact in LinkedIn groups.[61] With more than two million groups on LinkedIn,[62] there is no excuse not to join a group relevant to your industry or location. Eighty-one percent of users surveyed were in at least one LinkedIn group,[63] meaning networking contacts, hiring executives and recruiters—maybe even the one who will give you your dream job—are likely already members of, and might even be active in, a group. In a survey of LinkedIn users who found a job within three months of focused searching, 82 percent interacted with a group on LinkedIn.[64]

LinkedIn allows you to join fifty groups, so join those pertinent to your background, industry, and location. Determine a group's membership—larger ones offer more exposure. You will need to "apply" for membership to join a group.

Once you join a group, it is much easier to relate to people. You have something in common. Common ground is a good thing when starting a networking communication.

Groups send out routine updates to your email. Occasionally, job postings are contained in these emails. However, not all jobs posted

---

60 LinkHumans, "10 Tips."

61 Lindsey Pollak, "How to Attract Employers' Attention on LinkedIn," LinkedIn Blog, December 2, 2010, http://blog.linkedin.com/2010/12/02/find-jobs-on-linkedin/ (accessed June 4, 2015).

62 Arruda, William. "Is LinkedIn Poised To Be The Next Media Giant?" Forbes, March 8, 2015, http://www.forbes.com/sites/williamarruda/2015/03/08/is-linkedin-poised-to-be-the-next-media-giant/ (accessed June 5, 2015).

63 Pamela Vaughan, "81% of LinkedIn Users Belong to a LinkedIn Group [Data]," Hubspot Blogs, August 11, 2011, http://blog.hubspot.com/blog/tabid/6307/bid/22364/81-of-LinkedIn-Users-Belong-to-a-LinkedIn-Group-Data.aspx (accessed June 8, 2015).

64 Shreya Oswal, "7 Smart Habits of Successful Job Seekers [INFOGRAPHIC]," LinkedIn Blog, March 19, 2014, http://blog.linkedin.com/2014/03/19/7-smart-habits-of-successful-job-seekers-infographic/ (accessed June 9, 2015).

to these groups go out in the group's emails. Follow the job sections of your different groups for new job postings.

21. Contacts

Get dialed in—"the more contacts you have, the more likely you are to show up in the search results."[65] It's important to have the right kind of contacts—hiring executives, colleagues and peers in your industry, former employers, and so on. Generally speaking, look to connect with those who can help you, hire you, or both. Add people by searching for different keywords. These are the connections you want to have. You can also import your address book and connect with people you already know.

To distinguish yourself on LinkedIn, try to customize your request-for-connection message by writing a little about yourself and why you are interested in connecting. LinkedIn gives you a limited number of characters to do this, so be concise. Remember, first impressions are important, and this is your first impression.

Fully appreciate that your network has value and is an area of evaluation when others looks at your profile. An evaluation of the number of contacts in and quality of your network creates a "Network Value Score." By analogy, it's like your credit score when applying for a mortgage. The higher your "Network Value Score," the more valuable you may be perceived as a quality candidate for the position.

If you are new to LinkedIn or have been inactive, work to get five hundred connections. The number of connections you have appears on your profile until you exceed five hundred. After that, it appears as "500+." You want hiring executives viewing your profile to conclude that you have a network of professional colleagues. It can add to your professional value proposition. If you're staying within your field, it is not uncommon for hiring executives to see how many common connections you have with each other—the more the better. And, it is not uncommon for hiring executives to reach out to these

---

65 Frasco, "11 Tips."

common connections and inquire about you as well. Hence this is another good reason to stay active with your network.

22. Consider Upgrading Your Account

Consider upgrading your account to the premium level during your search. The prices are reasonable and the benefits are worth it. With a premium account, you can send InMails to reach more people on LinkedIn.[66] There are other advantages as well, including being able to see who's looked at your profile, how you compare to other applicants applying for the same position, coming up more often in searches, and so on.[67]

23. Job Alerts

LinkedIn can provide you job alerts for open positions based on past job searches you have performed. To receive these alerts, sign in to your LinkedIn account. Click on the Jobs tab on the front page, which will lead to a pop-up titled, "Jobs you may be interested in." Then click on "Get email alerts." Now you can choose how often you want to receive emails with new job information. When you look into seven jobs in one week, LinkedIn itself concludes that you are a job seeker. When that happens, you should automatically begin receiving emails from LinkedIn about jobs similar to the ones you researched.

24. Customize Your LinkedIn URL

Your current LinkedIn URL is likely your name, in lowercase letters, and possibly followed by a series of numbers, slashes, and so on. It can look rather technical. LinkedIn allows you to customize the URL to make it much more visually appealing. By customizing your

---

66 "InMail—Overview," LinkedIn Help Center, https://help.linkedin.com/app/answers/detail/a_id/1584/~/InMail---overview (accessed June 24, 2015).

67 Gyanda Sachdeva, "Unlocking Your Competitive Edge with the Power of LinkedIn Premium," LinkedIn Blog, December 18, 2014, http://blog.linkedin.com/2014/12/18/unlocking-your-competitive-edge-with-the-power-of-linkedin-premium/ (accessed June 9, 2015).

LinkedIn URL, it will be more appealing to the eye if you put it on your resume, business cards, and so forth.

The first thing to consider is what you want the customized URL to be. For many, it could be as simple as capitalizing your name, deleting the numbers, and leaving it at that. The programming on LinkedIn will either accept the change or give you three suggestions. It is acceptable to put a position title after your name (e.g., "JohnSmithengineer"). Or, a professional designation (e.g., "JohnSmithCEBS").[68] Or a branding word (e.g., "JohnSmithintegrity"). Just don't get carried away with this. Keep it simple. Here are the brief click-by-click steps:

- Go to your LinkedIn home page.

- Click on your small photo (or icon if you don't have a photo) at the far upper right-hand corner of the page. You'll get a drop-down menu.

- Click "Privacy and Settings."

- On this page under Settings (right column), click the link "Edit your public profile."

- On the upper right-hand section of the page, you'll see the option to change your URL. Click the little pencil icon and make your changes. You have between five and thirty letters or numbers—no spaces, symbols, or anything like that.

- Click "Save" and you're done.[69]

Remember, LinkedIn changes constantly, adding some features and functions and taking others away. Be aware of programming changes and their possible implications on your job search.

---

68 "Certified Employee Benefit Specialist"; see "About the CEBS Program," International Foundation of Employee Benefit Plans, Inc., https://www.ifebp.org/CEBSDesignation/overview/Pages/default.aspx (accessed November 12, 2015).

69 See also, Sue Cockburn, "Create Your Custom LinkedIn Web Address in 5 Easy Steps," *Growing Social Biz* (blog), September 30, 2015, http://growingsocialbiz.com/simple-steps-creating-your-customized-linkedin-url/ (accessed November 12, 2015).

Optimizing Your LinkedIn Profile

Now that we have discussed the sections of your LinkedIn profile, the goal is to maximize your exposure and get the most views possible. The ultimate goal is to have your profile appear on the first page of candidates when a hiring executive or recruiter puts a search criterion into LinkedIn. The following are five powerful tips to optimize your profile:

1. **Have a complete profile.** The first step to optimizing your profile is to have a complete profile and provide as much relevant professional information as you can. As you know, your profile is your online resume. It is often the first thing a hiring executive or recruiter views when searching for candidates or conducting an interview.

   LinkedIn ranks profile strength. To achieve the highest level, "All-Star," is not difficult. What makes your profile complete?

   a) Your industry and location

   b) An up-to-date, current position (with a description)

   c) Two past positions

   d) Your education

   e) Your skills (minimum of 3)

   f) A profile photo

   g) At least 50 connections[70]

2. **Add a photo.** As previously mentioned, having a photo results in fourteen times more views.[71] This statistic cannot be ignored. It is imperative in optimizing your LinkedIn profile to have a photo. It is highly recommended that the photo be professionally taken.

---

70 LinkedIn, "Profile Completeness."
71 Smith, "The Complete Guide."

3. **Keywords, keywords, keywords.** Populate your profile with keywords that apply to you. Include industry terms-of-art, abbreviations, and so on. Where these keywords appear does matter. *Keywords in your headline, summary, job title, career history, interests, and skills score highest.* Make sure these sections have the keywords you want to be known for or found for.[72] Be repetitious without going overboard. The more the keywords appear, the higher your potential ranking.

   The areas where most job seekers can improve their ranking is putting keywords in their headline, job title, and most notably in interests. For interests, include your business interests, not just personal interests, and be sure your business interests have keywords.

4. **Get recommendations.** Request recommendations from former bosses, customers, vendors, and colleagues. What others say about you is more impressive than what you say about yourself. The minimum recommended number is three (LinkedIn used to require three recommendations for an All-Star rating).[73]

   Many recruiters, when evaluating candidates on LinkedIn, look through recommendations. They look at the number and general comments. Reviewing recommendations has become a part of their evaluation process, and not having any can be a mark against you.

5. **Volunteering, Causes, Support.** According to LinkedIn, 42 percent of hiring executives surveyed indicated that volunteer experience is equal to formal work experience.[74] The sections in your profile where you can showcase your volunteer work and social consciousness are Volunteering Opportunities, Causes

---

72 Frasco, "11 Tips."

73 Donna Serdula, "LinkedIn's New Requirements for a 100% Complete Profile," LinkedIn Makeover (blog), February 20, 2012, http://www.linkedin-makeover.com/2012/02/20/linkedins-new-requirements-for-a-100-complete-profile/ (accessed November 5, 2015).

74 Dougherty, "16 Tips to Optimize."

You Care About, and Supported Organizations. Be sensitive and use your best judgment regarding any organizations or causes that could be viewed as controversial (politics, perhaps religion, and so on).

Following these five optimizing strategies will notably enhance your ranking when a hiring executive or recruiter searches for you on LinkedIn.

Test it. After you have revised your profile and optimized it, put it to the test. After making changes, wait a few minutes or a few hours to allow your revisions to make their way through the LinkedIn programming. Then get on LinkedIn (Use the Advanced search function on the top of the LinkedIn page next to the blue box with the spy glass) and conduct a keyword search for someone like you. You may also want to have a close friend run a search for you as well using the criteria you used to find yourself. How do you rank? Did you appear on the first page? On the first two or three pages? If not, look at the profiles that appeared on the first page and see if you can make improvements based on what those candidates put on their profiles. Selective borrowing is permitted. Make revisions and try it again. Do what you can to improve your ranking to appear on the first page or the first three pages.

Understand that there will be times that, regardless of the revisions you make and the optimizing strategies you use, you will only be able to improve your ranking so much. Do not go overboard! Your profile must still appear professional and informative. Optimizing is a great strategy, but creating an awkward-looking profile for ranking purposes defeats the ultimate objective . . . impressing a networking contact, hiring executive, or recruiter.

Make Your Profile Compelling

So far we have discussed the components of your LinkedIn profile—more than twenty boxes where you can put information about yourself. We have discussed the strategies to improve your ranking when a hiring executive or HR recruiter runs a search for someone like you. This is optimizing your profile in a nutshell.

Having information in your profile is step one. Getting found by optimizing your profile is step two. But the real test is making your profile compelling—a profile that *intellectually* and *emotionally* moves the viewer to contact you. You want the viewer to think, "I've got to talk to this person!"

Making your profile compelling drives straight to the heart of the substance of your career achievements. It's a matter of showcasing your knowledge, experience, and accomplishments. Whatever it is that makes you unique in your industry, you want it front and center so it cannot be missed. The point is to clearly announce (perhaps shamelessly announce) that you are qualified, good at what you do, and you've got the accomplishments to prove it!

Your unique qualifications and accomplishments can be put on display in several areas, such as your headline, summary, definitely in your experience section, and awards and honors.

Although superficial, consider putting icons in front of certain accomplishments or qualifications. These icons include bullet points, arrows, and so forth. Copy and paste them from other sources on the Internet and place them in front of an accomplishment or qualification. The icons draw the attention of the viewer.

The ultimate goal is to get discovered and impress the hiring executive or recruiter into contacting you. When they do, mission accomplished!

PART II

Professional Networking in a Job Search

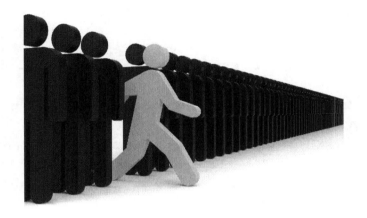

Everything you want is just outside your comfort zone.
— Robert Allen[75]

Hidden Job Market

As you network and engage the marketplace in search of a new job, accept this statistic: It is widely believed that "at least 70 percent, if not 80 percent, of jobs are not published."[76] These are often positions that get filled before a company has the need to advertise or post the

---

75 "Quotes on Initiative," *Leadership Now,* http://www.leadershipnow.com/initiativequotes. html (accessed May 28, 2015).

76 Kaufman, "A Successful Job Search."

opening online. These jobs are referred to as the "Hidden Job Market." Much has been written about the Hidden Job Market.[77] It is real. The Internet and social networking have dramatically changed the nature of job searching. As a result, networking techniques and strategies have taken on a whole new meaning.

Why do employers not advertise their open positions? For some, it is a matter of company policy that all job openings do get posted. However, many companies choose not to advertise for any of the following reasons:

The sheer amount of respondents (with the vast majority wholly unqualified) makes for time-consuming work sifting through countless applications and resumes.

For truly specialized positions, there are little or no qualified candidates.

Employers want well-qualified, interested, and affordable candidates without the hours of effort to locate them through advertising. This easing of the hiring process is part of the value recruiters bring to employers.

Some employers choose to fill positions by word of mouth and networking.

How can you tap the Hidden Job Market effectively and efficiently? Follow the networking strategies and techniques in this book. Take a proactive approach to your search (don't just sit at home and apply for jobs online). Network both online and face-to-face.

There is much more about networking in the following pages. But understand and appreciate this truth: Networking works, but it can take time. "Those who give . . . get" is said to be the philosophical foundation of effective networking.[78] When you help others find what they want, they will remember you and return the favor (persuasion principle of reciprocity).

---

77 *Get Hired Fast! Tap the Hidden Job Market in 15 Days* by Brian Graham, *Cracking the Hidden Job Market: How to Find Opportunity in Any Economy* by Donald Asher, and others.

78 Vlooten, Dick van. "The Seven Laws of Networking: Those Who Give, Get," *Career Magazine*, May 7, 2004, http://sciencecareers.sciencemag.org/career_magazine/previous_issues/articles/2004_05_07/nodoi.1275810282259244595 (accessed June 16, 2015).

Networking

Networking is an essential part of building wealth.
— Armstrong Williams[79]

Professional networking is developing and maintaining reciprocal relationships with other professionals that over time could result in career or business opportunities. The power of your network is measured by the number and quality of relevant relationships you have.[80]

Let's examine some of the important words and concepts in this definition:

Developing—Professional networks are not granted to you, they are built.

Maintaining—Once a professional connection or relationship is created, it must be nurtured. There must be some appropriate level of interaction.

Reciprocal relationships—Networking is a two-way street. The foundational concept of networking is to give or help. Each person in the relationship gives with the understanding that they can receive when the time is right. "Those who give . . . get."[81]

Measured by the number—To be useful or powerful, a network must be populated with enough contacts for your purposes.

Quality of relevant relationships—Your network must have the right kinds of connections. When your network has enough

---

79 Williams, Armstrong. "A Few Simple Steps to Building Wealth," *Townhall*, June 13, 2005, http://townhall.com/columnists/armstrongwilliams/2005/06/13/a_few_simple_steps_to_building_wealth/page/full (accessed May 28, 2015).

80 See also, Phillips, Simon. *The Complete Guide to Professional Networking: The Secrets of Online and Offline Success.* (London: Kogan Page Limited, 2014), p. 1.

81 Vlooten, "The Seven Laws."

quality, relevant relationships, it becomes truly powerful when properly used.

BusinessDictionary.com defines networking this way:

> Creating a group of acquaintances and associates and keeping it active through regular communication for mutual benefit. Networking is based on the question "How can I help?" and not with "What can I get?"[82]

The most important concept in this definition is offering to help. As we proceed in this book, we will examine and discuss steps you can take that fulfill these definitions and make you a skilled professional networker. Being skilled adds depth and quality to your network. You will be "going about it" in the right way. This will, in turn, shorten your job search.

Networking for a job involves connecting with people you know and then the people they know to lead you to a job. It also includes reaching out professionally to those you don't know for the same purpose.[83] It generally involves three types of contacts:

1. Those people who can lead you to others who can assist you in your job search.

2. Those people who can introduce you to someone who can hire you.

3. Those people with the authority to hire you.

Job search networking can take place in a wide variety of situations including face-to-face, online through professional networking sites (LinkedIn), social networking sites (Facebook and Twitter), professional associations, alumni events, and even the casual dinner gathering with friends.

82 "Networking," BusinessDictionary.com, http://www.businessdictionary.com/definition/networking.html (accessed November 12, 2015).

83 Claycomb, Heather, and Karl Dinse. *Career Pathways—Interactive Workbook.* (1995), Part 7.

In a job search context, networking increases your "find-ability." It is estimated that between 60 and 80 percent of all jobs are found by networking.[84] Furthermore, surveys indicate that job seekers who are referred to a hiring executive have a one in seven chance of landing a job offer compared to one in one hundred if they apply online.[85] Getting referred to a job is a function of networking. So, statistically speaking, your next job will come as a result of your networking efforts.

This next concept is very important and goes straight to the heart of professionally networking for a job: It's not how many people you know, but rather how many people know you. Ponder that for a moment to understand the concept. How many people do you know well enough that they would refer you to someone else or possibly go out of their way to help you, even if it's in a small measure? It's this kind of relationship networking that drives a job search.

Networking Philosophies

The general consensus among networking experts is there are three philosophies people adopt when building networks. They are closed, open, and selective.[86]

A closed networking approach is very restrictive. It generally includes only those connections you personally have met and like, giving some room for general acquaintances.

An open networking approach is the exact opposite. It's a "come one, come all" approach. This approach is exemplified by those who designate themselves as LinkedIn Open Networkers or LION.[87]

---

84 LinkedIn, "Using LinkedIn to Find a Job"; Beatty, "The Math Behind the Networking Claim"; Rothberg, "80% of Job Openings."

85 Jobvite, "Jobvite Social Recruiting Survey Finds Over 90% of Employers Will Use Social Recruiting in 2012," news release, July 9, 2012, http://www.jobvite.com/press-releases/2012/jobvite-social-recruiting-survey-finds-90-employers-will-use-social-recruiting-2012/ (accessed November 10, 2015).

86 Phillips, *Guide to Professional Networking*, p. 17–22.

87 Ibid., p. 19.

The third approach is selective. As the name implies, you choose who to connect with based on criteria that the potential connection must meet.

All of these approaches are valid depending upon your personal and professional purposes for your network. We'll briefly discuss the benefits and drawbacks of each approach as it applies to your professional network and your job search.

A closed network is generally small and normally not any bigger than a few hundred contacts—many of whom you have a close or long-standing relationship with. This network can be valuable in a job search if you live in a smaller city or the connections are high-quality influencers. The drawback is the network is not expansive enough to reach deeply into the hidden job market. There are simply not enough connections to provide enough referrals or job leads.

An open network can be very large as it grows over time. Open networks can grow into the thousands, tens of thousands, and more. Once developed, such a network can be a rich source of information, referrals, and job leads. However, a large open network can become unmanageable, the level of your relationships can be superficial at best, and overall quality tends to diminish. These drawbacks may significantly reduce the usefulness of the network for your job search.

A selective network approach blends the closed and open approaches by applying professional criteria to each potential connection. Before a contact is "accepted for membership" in the network, the contact must meet the membership criteria—which you establish.

There are several advantages to this approach. It helps keep the quality of your network high. It is populated only by those connections who meet your criteria. It is more manageable in size and therefore easier for you to develop and maintain relationships. The connections tend to be more closely related by common industries, functions, or location. This can elevate your professional stature (and perceived influence) with others in your network as they discover who you are connected to.

The networking philosophy you adopt in building your job search network is a personal choice. That decision rests on the role your network will play in your job search, your career, and business in general.

Embrace a Networking Mentality

To successfully network for a job (or in business generally), it is imperative that you embrace several attitudes to make your efforts effective. They include:

Being Sincere—A skilled professional networker shows genuine interest in relationships and communication with others. That means taking the time to have meaningful engagements properly gauged by the depth of the relationships. This could mean a thirty-minute conversation or a brief exchange of emails.

Being Helpful—This goes straight to the heart of proper professional networking. Offer to help. Give others what they need and they will try to return the favor (persuasion principle of reciprocity). Always be on the lookout to provide value to others whenever you can, with the expectation of receiving nothing in return. Rewards will come as the level of trust and rapport grows. You'll also learn what is of interest to your connections. If you discover an item (an article, referral, or business lead, among many others) that you feel confident would have substantial value to your connection, pass it along to them.

Staying Present—As you network, be present in the moment. Whether interacting face-to-face, by telephone, or online, give your undivided attention to your contact.

Listening—The best networkers do one thing very well: they listen. They quiet themselves, are present in the moment, and listen to learn. The more you listen and ask questions, the more rapport you build. This creates or adds to the value of the relationship. By actively listening, you will often learn what others need so you can help them.

Having a Positive Attitude—Always approach your networking with a positive attitude. People enjoy being around those who are positive and have an optimistic view of life. Your connections will want to engage with you and look forward to doing so. Nobody wants to talk to a "sad sack."

Having Patience and Playing for the Long Term—Approach networking as an investment that will grow in value over time. Done correctly, it can pay dividends for the life of your career.

Following up—Following up after an engagement is critical to the development of the relationship. Timely and professional follow-up will differentiate you from others and elevate your status in the mind of your contact.[88]

When you embrace these attitudes toward networking, you'll approach every step and every networking communication with the right frame of mind. You will develop more quality relevant relationships faster that will last longer, potentially for your entire career.

Fear of Networking

Unfortunately, many job seekers hesitate to take full advantage of networking because they're intimidated or are afraid of being viewed as pushy, annoying, or self-serving. Put those feelings aside. Networking is not about arrogant self-promotion. Instead, it's about building relationships. When you think about networking as building relationships—or creating professional friendships—many of your fears will disappear.[89]

Accept this next statement as gospel truth: Whether your networking is formal or informal, online or offline, there are people out there who want to help. It's your job to get out there and let them!

---

88 See also, ibid., Chapter 4, "How to Work the Room in Five Easy Steps."
89 Ibid., p. 1.

Do the thing you fear, and the death of fear is certain.
— Emerson[90]

Why Networking Is So Effective

There are several reasons why networking is an effective way to find your next opportunity:

1. **It taps into the Hidden Job Market.**

2. **It decreases the time it takes to land a new position.** Networking is a proactive job search tactic. People you know or have been referred to are more likely to speak or meet with you personally. And, the more communications you have, the closer you get to a job offer.

3. **It reduces competition.** Job postings tend to draw a pile of resumes. Networking makes you the preferred candidate of a much smaller candidate pool.

4. **It introduces you through a common connection and expands your current network.** People do business primarily with people they know and like.[91] As your network expands, so will your opportunities as you meet more and more people.

5. **It helps you practice for interviews and builds self-confidence.** Networking creates phone conversations, lunch dates, and research interviews. These are opportunities to practice your interview skills. This will boost your self-confidence, awareness that your job search is moving forward, and feelings of success as you improve overall, leading to better interviews. Having confidence translates

---

90 "Ralph Waldo Emerson Quotable Quote," Goodreads, www.goodreads.com/quotes/60285-do-the-thing-you-fear-and-the-death-of-fear (accessed May 28, 2015).

91 Byrne, Attraction, quoted in Kurtzberg and Naquin, *Essentials*, p. 35.

into better communications, which creates more interviews, eventually leading to more job opportunities.[92]

Types of Networks

Conceptually there are two job search networks: personal and professional. Your personal network includes family, friends, neighbors, and doctors, as well as your dentist, financial advisor, accountant, and members of church, civic, or philanthropic groups you attend. Everyone else you interact with in your personal life is also included here. Websites in your personal network include Facebook and Twitter, among others.

Your professional network is developed from your career and consists of people who are work colleagues, connections at other companies, former bosses, senior management, association contacts, and so on. The leading online site for professional networks is LinkedIn.

Both networks can be extremely powerful in directing you and connecting you to potential job opportunities. Deciding which network will yield the most leads is personal and depends upon your circumstances. Your networks could perform equally well.

Each one of your contacts connects you to their network. And any member of that network could know about an available opportunity. Let's say you have solid relationships with twenty people in either your personal or professional network. Now let's say they each know twenty people. That's four hundred people you can get to know reasonably quickly without much effort.

For some people, twenty connections is a very low number. It's possible that your network, especially on the professional side, could be in the hundred-plus range. You do the math on how large your extended network could be—chances are, you'll be pleasantly surprised.

---

92 Moynihan et al., "A Longitudinal Study," quoted in Kurtzberg and Naquin, *Essentials*, p. 30–32.

Evaluating the Strength and Quality of Your Network

Prior to actively networking, take some time and evaluate your current network. Are there enough quality, relevant contacts to drive your job search efforts?

Give yourself one point for each of the following questions that you answer yes:

1. Is your professional network comprised predominantly of people within your industry or position type?

2. Does it contain connections who can lead you to other connections who have influence, perhaps even potential hiring executives?

3. Do you feel your professional network is large enough?

4. Are you a member of enough industry-specific LinkedIn groups, associations, or relevant local groups?

5. Do you feel your network can help you?

How did you do?

5 points: Great job on your network!

4 points: Your network is excellent, but could stand some improvement.

3 points: You need to spend time building your network.

2 points: Your network needs serious attention.

0 or 1 point: Get your network a lifeline, stat!

If you need to improve your network, put in extra time and effort to get introduced and connected to others who can enhance the strength and quality of your contact base. The more time and effort you devote to your network, the quicker it will grow . . . and the quicker you'll connect with your next opportunity.

Create Your Professional "Cabinet"

The President of the United States has a Cabinet. It is a select group of trusted advisors composed of the Vice President and the heads of the executive departments of government, totaling sixteen (not including others who are a part at the President's discretion).[93] You also need to create a Cabinet of trusted advisors. Here is a definition to guide your thinking, selection, and development process:

> A professional (networking) Cabinet is a select group of people in your professional life whom you can trust and call upon knowing that they will undoubtedly help you in any way reasonably possible. This would include providing you with advice, introductions, mentorship/"tough love," referrals, insight, and recommendations, among other things. It is a reciprocal relationship for which they know they can count on you for the same.

Let's examine a few components of the definition:

A select group—Your Cabinet will likely be small, comprising five to ten people, perhaps a few more if you can create and maintain close relationships. It's likely that your Cabinet will be people with whom you have developed (or are currently developing) a close relationship.

Professional life—Your Cabinet is a group of people in your professional life. These people may be your friends, but the foundation of the relationship started in your professional life.

Trust—These people must be trustworthy. They are, in large part, confidants to whom you can be vulnerable regarding professional matters.

Undoubtedly help—These are people you can count on and who have your best interests at heart. These people are your "go-to" inner circle.

---

93 "Constitutional Topic: The Cabinet," U.S. Constitution Online, http://www.usconstitution. net/consttop_cabi.html (accessed November 10, 2015).

In any way reasonably possible—You must understand and appreciate that there are limits. In the President's Cabinet, each member has an area of expertise. This is also true with your Cabinet. Your Cabinet will likely consist of professionals who have unique abilities, insight, connections, and so on. In fact, over time you want to have a reasonably diverse Cabinet.

A reciprocal relationship—As with any network, the relationship must be a two-way street to be productive. You must be willing to give when your fellow Cabinet member needs you.

A Cabinet is a very important networking group to create and have. It is the group you can rely upon in a pinch. They are your network's foundation. How many people do you know who you can contact almost immediately and ask for help with full confidence that you will receive it? If that number is not at least five to ten, you need to grow your Cabinet.

Create Your Sales Company

The next layer of your network is your "Sales Company." The words used to describe these network contacts were chosen by design.

Sales. As you know, salespeople promote the products and services of the employer. They sell the benefits of those products and services. They assist buyers. They are ambassadors for their employers in the market. They also provide market intelligence and feedback to their employer. By analogy, you want to create a layer of connections who will assist you, promote you, be your ambassador in the job market when given an opportunity, and provide you market intelligence and feedback.

These are the people you have good professional and collegial relationships with. You have interacted with them professionally, and perhaps socially, at some level. These are people you are reasonably sure (though not completely, like your Cabinet) will help or provide a lending hand if the opportunity presents itself. Put into percentages, your Cabinet is 100 percent sure to help. Your Sales Company is 60 percent and above. It's more likely than not. There are no scientific percentages, but connections in your Sales Company are those people you can call on who are likely to help. This help can range from:

> "I'll keep my eyes open."

> "You might want to read this article on XYZ Company."

> "You may want to network with Kipp Sawyer."

> "Call Ruth Moore, my boss. We're looking!"

Always be a professional networker and thank everyone who responds and offer to help them if they need anything.

Company. The word "company" is chosen for its military definition. A military company is one hundred to two hundred soldiers.[94] Therefore, picking the midpoint, your Sales Company should number around 150 contacts. The 150 number also has some scientific basis—it happens to be the Dunbar Number, created by British anthropologist Robin Dunbar. Based on his studies, he theorized that there is a numerical limit to the number of individuals with whom a stable interpersonal relationship can be maintained. That number is 150.[95]

The point is this: You want to have around 150 connections in your Sales Company.

Let's think through the power of what this could mean for your job search. Let's assume that you have a healthy network—ten Cabinet members and 150 in your Sales Company. Now, let's assume that only 40 percent of your Sales Company actually provides assistance

---

94 "Operational Unit Diagrams," United States Army, http://www.army.mil/info/organization/unitsandcommands/oud/ (accessed November 10, 2015).

95 Konnikova, Maria. "The Limits of Friendship," *The New Yorker*, October 7, 2014, http://www.newyorker.com/science/maria-konnikova/social-media-affect-math-dunbar-number-friendships (accessed November 10, 2015).

to you in some form (remember the 60 percent number—so we are being pessimistic about the level of help for this example). Let's do the math: 40 percent of 150 is sixty, plus ten (Cabinet members are 100 percent reliable) gets you to seventy. You have seventy sales reps, advisors, promoters, and ambassadors out there helping you and promoting you in some measure. Think about that for a moment . . . that's a lot! Are you beginning to grasp the importance and power of a healthy network?

The Peripheral and Pruning

Outside your Cabinet and your Sales Company are the rest of your connections: the people you know, are acquainted with, or simply connected to on LinkedIn. They are peripheral but still important!

All human relationships ebb and flow. People enter your life and stay or fade away over time for any one of a thousand reasons. This will be true with your network. The people in your network will migrate between or out of your network circles. Cabinet members move to the Sales Company and vice versa. Some retire or pass away. New connections appear on the scene. Maintain and cultivate relationships and be aware of what you have with your Cabinet and Sales Company.

Then there are times when you need to prune your network. This is when the relationship with the connection has diminished in value to a point where there is no mutual (professional) benefit for the relationship. It would be like a director of robotics being connected to a person who has become a pastry chef. The connection is just not there, at least not on a professional level. From a job search perspective, these would be connections who can neither hire you, help you, nor be a center of influence for you.

On LinkedIn, these are the connections you may choose to "remove." When you do this, the connection is not alerted that you have severed the connection. And, more often than not, your circle of professional acquaintances is or has become divergent enough that it will go completely unnoticed. There'll be no hard feelings.

Building Your Professional Network (ICE Method)

It's not what you know, but who you know.
— Unknown[96]

The process of building or enhancing your current professional network is filled with fun, gratification, and challenges. It is exhilarating and special when you connect with someone new or reconnect with someone from your past. It can be equally disappointing when you can't connect with a desirable contact or when your networking efforts don't produce the results you'd like.

The process of building your professional network can be broken down into three steps, with the steps being interchangeable depending upon the circumstances. They are Identify, Connect, and Engage (ICE).

Identify

From a job search perspective, there are three categories of professionals you want to reach out to and connect with. They are:

1. Those people who can lead you to others who can assist you in your job search.

2. Those people who can introduce you to someone who can hire you.

3. Those people with the authority to hire you.

---

96 Popik, Barry. "It's not what you know, but who you know," The Big Apple, October 9, 2009, http://www.barrypopik.com/index.php/new_york_city/entry/its_not_what_you_know_but_who_you_know/ (accessed November 10, 2015).

So, who are these people you should reach out to and connect with?

1. People who can lead you to others who can assist you in your job search. This could include a wide variety of contacts depending upon your unique circumstances and job search. These could be contacts in civic, philanthropic, fundraising, and other sectors who by function of their job or volunteer work would be a good source. This is an excellent technique for local job searches.

2. Within your industry, these could be professionals with the same or similar title and function as your own.[97] They are your peers. They could be with target employers of interest to you. These are people who hear about openings and can pass that information along to you.

3. Professionals who are one to two titles or functions above your own.[98] These are the professionals or executives who can either hire you or influence the hiring decision. They may know other executives at other companies who have openings or introduce you to them for further networking.

4. People with similar and higher titles and functions than your own with companies that routinely interact with target employers or within a target industry of interest to you. These connections can serve two purposes. First, they may hear about opportunities with companies directly within your industry or from target employers. Second, they may seek to hire you and capitalize upon your abilities and skills in a different way. Having these contacts could open your career in a direction you had not before considered.[99]

---

97 Yate, *Knock 'em Dead*, p. 83.

98 See also, ibid.

99 See also, ibid.

There are several sources you can use to identify potential connections. Some rich resources include:

- Industry conference attendees' lists
- Industry association membership lists
- Members of LinkedIn Groups

The next steps are often interchangeable depending upon how the relationship is initiated.

Connect

There are a variety of ways you can connect with your identified target contacts. Professional and social networking sites have made this process much easier. We'll delve into the "how to" steps in just a moment. Suffice it to say, you can ask to connect on LinkedIn, follow them on Twitter, and so on. The goal of connecting (for the purposes of this step) is to have a means of direct communication with your contact.

Making the Connection through LinkedIn: Referral

The most effective way to make a connection is by referral. Getting referred by a common connection instantaneously establishes a level of trust. Your introduction is grounded in the persuasion principle of social proof and functions as an endorsement.

Once you have identified a target contact, search through LinkedIn and see if you have common connections. Reach out to one (perhaps two) and request an introduction. Below is an email (or InMail) template you can modify for your purposes:

Subject Line: Introduction of [your name] to [target's name]

Hi _____,

I trust this message finds you well! [Add a second sentence as appropriate, e.g., "How's that little quarterback of yours?"]

I need a favor. I would like to get introduced to [target's name], and I see that you are connected on LinkedIn. [The next sentence should state the general purpose for the introduction. For example, "I am researching companies for a possible career move, and I would like to speak with him/her about (name of company)." What you are asking for is a research interview, which is explained later.] If you are comfortable doing so and believe the introduction would be well received, I would appreciate it. If not, no worries.

Best Regards,
[Your name]
[Telephone number]

Always provide your telephone number so the common connection can call and ask questions.

Direct Request
You can also ask the target contact to join your LinkedIn network directly. Avoid the standard "invite" whenever possible. Instead, customize your requests to connect. Below are some ways to relate to your target contact to improve the chances that your invitation is accepted:

- Refer to a common connection by name (especially when you know they have a good relationship).
- Refer to a common industry association.
- Refer to a common or several common LinkedIn groups.

- Refer to the number of common connections (at least ten or more to make this approach effective).

LinkedIn only gives you a limited number of words or characters for your invite. Be concise!

Below is a template to get you started:

Hi Linda,

I am a [identify your function or title], and we are both members of the [name of group] LinkedIn group. In fact, we have over ten common connections! I'd like you to be a part of my network on LinkedIn.

Thanks,

Jean

The target contact's initial impression of your invitation and the type of networks he/she has will determine whether your invitation is accepted.

Traditional Email Approach

Reaching out to a target networking contact can naturally be done through traditional email. Unlike using LinkedIn, which limits the number of words or characters for an invite, traditional email allows you more space and latitude. When composing your email, keep these guidelines in mind:

Subject line: This is important. It is the first thing the reader sees. Try to create a subject line that will motivate the contact to open and read the email.

Greeting: You have a decision to make regarding the greeting. Do you use "Rich" or "Mr. Higgs?" Using a proper prefix (Mr., Ms., or something else) automatically elevates the contact and formalizes the opening moments of the relationship. Using the first name creates more of a peer-like relationship. One suggestion to address this issue is to use informal first names for peers and contacts one level above you and formal prefixes for others. The decision is ultimately yours based on your professional judgment.

Relate: Whenever possible, reference something in common. See the list in the previous section.

Compliment: If possible, state a sincere compliment about the contact or company. The compliment must be genuine and substantive. If you find yourself stretching to say something substantive, bypass the compliment idea.

Identify yourself and state your purpose: Move to the heart of the matter. State the reason you are reaching out. Think elevator speech for starters.

State an accomplishment: Mention your most notable achievement (just one).

Ask for assistance, advice: This is your call to action. State what you are asking for, even if it is just to connect. Never ask for a job.

Keep it concise: Write what needs to be written. Get to the point and be done.

Signature block: This is your name, email address (even though they have it from the email), and telephone number.[100]

Here's an example:

Subject Line: Referred to you by Tim Fischer

Rich,

Tim Fischer suggested I reach out to you. Tim informed me that SyncHealth is growing rapidly. Congratulations!

I am a sales management executive, and my forte is training and

---

100 Pete Leibman, "9 Keys on How to Email a New Networking Contact During a Job Search," *CareerMuscles* (blog), January 6, 2011, https://careermuscles.wordpress.com/2011/01/06/9-keys-on-how-to-email-a-new-networking-contact-during-a-job-search-written-by-career-expert-pete-leibman/ (accessed November 10, 2015).

mentoring sales professionals. Over the course of my career, my sales teams have met or exceeded their group production goals more than 85 percent of the time.

I'm looking to make a career move to an organization that needs sales leadership to grow sales and market share.

I would like to connect with you for any insight you may have regarding [choose a topic] and any advice for my job search.

I know your time is limited, so I want to thank you in advance.

Best Regards,
Max Arteberry
m.arteberry@domainname.com
123-456-7890

Engage

Once you have connected, you need to engage in communication with your contact. This could take several forms, including a face-to-face meeting, a telephone call, a video conference or Skype call, or an exchange of emails. Let your judgment be your guide on the most appropriate form of communication. The goal of the engagement is to build rapport, explore common interests, and establish trust (not "ask for a job"). Completely establishing a foundation of trust during the first engagement likely will not happen. This takes time. You want to put the building blocks in place for the creation of a professional relationship.

As mentioned, it is entirely possible that steps two and three could be reversed, depending upon circumstances. For example, you might meet someone at a conference (engagement) and formalize the connection later on LinkedIn.[101]

---

101 Phillips, *Guide to Professional Networking*, Chapter 4, "How to Work the Room in Five Easy Steps."

How to Start a Face-to-Face Networking Conversation

Starting a networking conversation with a new contact from a "dead stop" can feel intimidating and awkward, especially when your target contact is a desirable one. These feelings can be compounded if the contact is a level or more in title above your own. Such anxiety is completely normal. Fortunately, that can be significantly reduced by following the suggestions and techniques below.

We are going to divide this topic between starting a networking conversation with a target contact (someone you select to reach out to) and an impromptu or general networking conversation with someone you simply happen to meet (usually at a conference or event).

Starting a Networking Conversation
with a Target Contact

The key to making a strong first impression with a target contact is to do your homework. Research the contact's background and career track. Look for commonalities of any kind that can be mentioned to build rapport. Mention personal or company accomplishments. Beginning with a sincere compliment can help start the flow of conversation.

Research the contact's company. This includes the website, news releases, and annual report, among other sources. Look for issues you can solve or initiatives of the company that you can assist or improve.

This research and preparation is very important. What you learn will give you conversation topics of interest to the contact. It shows that you did your homework and indicates to the contact that the conversation will be substantive—not just small talk.

Starting an Impromptu Networking Conversation with an Unknown Contact

It is inevitable that you will encounter situations where you are introduced to or simply find yourself with an unknown contact. You have no idea whether the contact could be "high value" or just social.

The key to success with these contacts is to be proactive. Ask the first question! Get the contact talking about themselves, their company, role, circumstances, and more. From this information, you can evaluate the circumstances and make a determination about how you will handle the conversation. Ask the first question and make sure it is open ended so you can gather information.

Here are a few conversation starters and topics:

- "So, what do you do?"
- "Tell me about your company."
- "What drew you to attend the [event/function]?"
- Pick an industry trend and seek an opinion or ask how it has affected their company.

First Impressions

Research has repeatedly shown that people heavily base their evaluations on their initial impressions.[102] Therefore, the first thirty to sixty seconds of your engagement are crucial to your success. Just like an interviewer, your networking contact creates first impressions of you—positive or negative—in that quick snippet of time.[103]

If the networking contact draws a negative first impression,

---

102 Zolfagharifard, Ellie. "First Impressions Really DO Count: Employers Make Decisions About Job Applicants in Under Seven Minutes," *Daily Mail*, June 18, 2014, http://www.dailymail.co.uk/sciencetech/article-2661474/First-impressions-really-DO-count-Employers-make-decisions-job-applicants-seven-minutes.html (accessed June 5, 2015).

103 Regis University Career Services, "Interviewing Strategies for CPS Students and Alumni," Regis University, http://www.regis.edu/About-Regis-University/University-Offices-and-Services/Career-Services/Student-and-Alumni/Interviewing-Strategies.aspx (accessed June 19, 2015).

there is a tendency to show disinterest. Or that person could elect to minimize the engagement or cut it short.

On the other hand, if a positive first impression is made, there is a tendency to engage in more meaningful conversation.

Create an initial positive impression by dressing conservatively (over 50 percent of a person's impression of you is determined by physical appearance),[104] smiling, having a firm handshake, and by making opening remarks that demonstrate your sincere interest in meeting the contact. Creating an initial positive impression creates an environment for a positive engagement.

If you believe you may not have made a positive first impression, you have some work to do, but you can recover.[105] Here are a couple of things you can do. First, ask questions about the contact, his or her company, and focus on questions about them. Second, name-drop if you can (capitalizing on the persuasion principle of liking and perhaps social proof). If you know that this person and you have someone in common, mention the name. That might be enough to redirect the dialogue into positive territory. Even if your performance is superior, you may not overcome that initial negative impression. However, do what you can to recover the best you can. Another opportunity to speak with the networking contact may present itself where you can improve upon the situation.

Goals of a Networking Conversation

Your primary goal in a networking conversation is to display and utilize professional networking techniques. Yes, you are networking with the purpose of advancing your job search, but you will gain

---

104 Jamal, Nina, and Judith Lindenberger. "How to Make a Great First Impression," *Business Know-How*, http://www.businessknowhow.com/growth/dress-impression.htm (accessed June 2, 2015).

105 "Cognitive scientists say it can take up to two hundred times the amount of information to undo a first impression as it takes to make one." Zack, Devora. "10 Tips for People Who Hate Networking," Careerealism, May 4, 2015, http://www.careerealism.com/hate-networking-tips/ (accessed July 17, 2015).

more traction and advance your search further by being patient and strategic.

Display networking skills first: be present in the moment, actively listen, ask questions, offer insight, and so on. Avoid a statement of your situation until the contact asks a question about you. By using your professional networking skills and engaging in conversation, you have built rapport. Then, when you state your situation, there is more likelihood the contact will help you!

Listen carefully and learn—what you discover may help advance your job search (you never know). You could also pass on to others what you discover and possibly help them in a myriad of ways.

Record Important Information

Proactively engage. Encourage dialogue by asking open-ended questions. Listen and learn. Then, after the conversation, record important information on the back of a business card or in a notebook. Write it down so you can remember the important information and follow up as circumstances may dictate.

Exiting a Networking Conversation

In every networking conversation there comes natural points to conclude the engagement. Never overstay or artificially extend a conversation, especially with a high-interest contact. Here are a few things to remember when wrapping up a networking conversation with a desirable contact:

- Exchange contact information. This will likely be done with business cards.

- Restate any follow-up steps either party has indicated will be taken. If you obligate yourself to follow up on a specific action item, do so and be timely! Record it somewhere so you do not forget.

- Finally, be a professional networker and follow networking protocol . . . ask if there is anything you can do for the contact (beyond what you may have already committed). If your contact is also a professional networker, he/she will recognize this and it will elevate you and improve the impression the contact has of you.

Then there are those times when the conversation has run its course and you feel stuck. In these situations, you'll need to show a couple of minutes of patience then gracefully exit (escape?) the conversation. Here are a few techniques you can use:

- Indicate to the contact that both of you have others to meet and catch up with. Exchange contact information and politely say you look forward to speaking again later.

- Indicate to the contact that you just identified someone you need to speak with. Politely ask to be excused, exchange contact information, and say you look forward to speaking again.

- Invite and introduce another contact (or two) into the conversation. Once their dialogue begins, excuse yourself. The key to this approach is to show a few moments of patience, if possible. Exiting too quickly could leave the impression that you've dumped the contact on others.

Learning to fluidly and gracefully enter and exit conversations is a valuable networking skill that, with practice, will produce tremendous results.

Follow Up

Always follow up after every substantive engagement with a contact! Too many job seekers diminish their networking efforts by failing to take the necessary time to follow up.

The follow-up communication can take a variety of forms. It could be:

1. An email or InMail simply expressing your appreciation or enjoyment of the communication.

2. A call or voicemail.

3. Providing information you indicated you would.

4. Providing something of value to the connection (by email attachment, US Mail, or special delivery).

The above list is certainly not exhaustive. Use your professional judgment in your follow-up communications. Remember, following up after an engagement is critical to the development of the relationship. It differentiates you from others, elevates your status in the mind of the contact, and will advance your job search.

Evaluating Your Networking Efforts

When evaluating your networking efforts, be very cautious about measuring success by the end result you want—job leads, interviews, or offers. Those are the wrong criteria for evaluating your networking efforts.

Rather, measure your networking by the intangibles. Focus your attention on the quality of your outreaches, the quality of your connections, the quality of your communications, your ability to provide value to others, and so on. Measure yourself by asking these questions:

- Am I sincere, caring, and demonstrating interest when I communicate?

- Have I been helpful or offered to help?

- Have I been present and focused during a conversation, giving my contact undivided attention?

- Am I listening to understand the content of the conversation and perhaps empathize with the contact?
- Am I smiling and showing optimism?
- Am I providing value when I can?
- Am I following up?[106]

These are the proper measurements to evaluate your networking efforts. If you are answering yes to these questions, your networking is effective, you're showing others your professionalism, and the rewards will come!

Additional Thoughts About LinkedIn

We previously discussed how to create a LinkedIn profile. Here are some additional networking strategies to keep in mind regarding LinkedIn:

1. **Use good judgment when connecting or extending invitations.** Determine whether a potential connection could be helpful or a center of influence for you. Connect with those who are in your industry or field of interest.

   Extend invitations to peers in your industry and those one to two levels above your title or function. Going above two levels may stretch the logical relevance of connecting.[107]

   If you extend an invitation that is not accepted, it's okay. Try not to take it personally. Instead, create an Excel spreadsheet of those who did not respond with a hyperlink to their profile. If you upgraded your LinkedIn account, you can still reach this person for future communication as needed or appropriate.

2. **Join Groups.** As previously mentioned, there are over two

---

106 Phillips, *Guide to Professional Networking*, 117–119.

107 See also, Yate, *Knock 'em Dead*, p. 83.

million LinkedIn groups.[108] Statistically, there are groups that will apply to you—join them.

Once you are in a group, it is easier to connect and get introduced to people of interest to you. Whenever possible, customize your invitation for a better response and success rate.

3. **Follow target companies.** Look up the company page for any company you are interested in. Click the "Follow Company" tab. All activity from that company's page, including job postings, will appear on your LinkedIn home page. This is a great feature to track the company's activities and potential hiring needs.

4. **Use the "Discover Jobs in Your Network" feature.** LinkedIn now informs you of job openings at companies where you have LinkedIn connections. If a position becomes available that interests you, see if you can get a referral from someone you know who works for the employer.

LinkedIn conducted a six-month study of senior level professionals (Vice President titles and above) and their use of LinkedIn during their job search. The results clearly indicated that these senior level professionals knew "the value of building and nurturing professional relationships in order to be successful in their job search"[109] (networking). The study found that "80 percent were sending connection requests, 50 percent were participating in groups, 40 percent were engaging on LinkedIn via shares, likes, and comments."[110]

Do your best to keep track of changes to LinkedIn's system, as these changes could affect your profile (and job search as a whole).

---

108 Arruda, "Is LinkedIn Poised."
109 Ayele, "Land Your Dream Job."
110 Ibid.

Spreading the Word—Asking for Help

Having access to a network will not help you find a job until you get the word out about your situation. Start by making contact with your strong connections (your Cabinet). Initial contact can be either by email or by telephone. A personal call is always best even if it is a follow-up to an email (or LinkedIn InMail).

Focus your networking on connecting and exchanging information. This enhances or builds a relationship that, over time, becomes mutually beneficial. Maintaining professional friendships is a give-and-take process. Take time to catch up on family, mutual friends, industry trends, and so on, if a connection is strong. After that, segue to the topic of your job search. Do not ask for a job (especially if your connection is in a position to hire). Trust in the fact that if your connection can hire you or refer you to someone who can, they will. Instead, enlist your contact as an information source, ally, or a lookout for your job search. Ask for information, insight, and advice.

Be as specific as possible about the type of position, company, or industry you are interested in. Aimless or generic networking requests are often vague, and your networking contact will struggle to remember what you need. Providing specific information is easier for your networking contact to remember—and to recall that it was you.

When reaching out to a new connection, inform him/her how you are connected. Use a referral's name or common association membership whenever possible. Then, with humble sincerity, professionally inform the connection of your situation. Like a strong connection, enlist this new connection as an information source or lookout for your job search. Don't forget to provide this person with your contact information.

If you are unemployed, consider sending your resume to your connection if given permission to do so. In your cover email, restate or inform the connection of the types of opportunities you would be interested in. Do not include any salary information. Grant permission for the connection to pass along your resume to others if it would be appropriate, in their opinion, to do so.

For every connection you make, be sensitive to their time. Make the connection, have the conversation, but do not overextend your conversation. You will know when it is time to wrap it up. Boring or over-informing a connection does not help your job search.

Networking in a Local Market for a Local Position

For local, general (non-industry-specific) job searches, network with those who are dependent upon networking for their livelihood. These people include real estate agents, financial planners, stockbrokers, mortgage lenders, bankers, and insurance agents, among others. These people interact with the public every day and frequently are privy to information from these interactions that could lead to a job opportunity.

Another group to network with are those involved in civic organizations, and philanthropic and fundraising activities. These people often interact with local business leaders and hear about certain openings.

Maintaining Your Network

To network successfully, remember that you are building mutually beneficial relationships. That means giving freely to others, as well as receiving. Try to give without the expectation of receiving whenever appropriate. Nurture these relationships. Avoid being a hit-and-run networker, disappearing after you get what you want.[111] With an appropriate level of communication, you will create a network that will benefit you and your network for years to come, perhaps a lifetime.

---

111 "Job Networking Tips," HelpGuide.org, http://www.helpguide.org/articles/work-career/job-networking-tips.htm (accessed November 3, 2015).

Keeping Momentum in Networking

As you can see, networking is an ongoing process. After an initial flurry of activity in making easy contacts, you may feel your momentum slowing. Make it a priority to network every day in some form. Reach out. Talk with someone, preferably someone new. A good goal is to network with someone new every day (or five new people in the course of a week). You will be pleasantly surprised how your network will grow. Remember, networking is how most jobs are found.[112]

Professional Associations

Professional associations are one of the most powerful networking tools you have. One of the best things you can do to shorten your job search is to join and be (reasonably) active in a professional association. Associations exist to promote the interests of the industry it serves and the careers of its members—through networking!

Some of the most connected and networked professionals you'll ever meet will belong to professional associations. These people get a "charge" out of being connected in your industry. So, as you discover them, connect with them, network with them, and (professionally and diplomatically) leverage them as a resource for your job search.[113]

Professional associations are mostly volunteer organizations. With the exception of a select few positions in large national associations, an association depends on its members volunteering to help. This is achieved through various committees tasked with certain functions. With your job search in mind, which committees could bear the most fruit from networking? Two committees in particular can be most helpful:

---

112 LinkedIn, "Using LinkedIn to Find a Job"; Beatty, "The Math Behind the Networking Claim"; Rothberg, "80% of Job Openings."

113 Yate, *Knock 'em Dead*, p. 86.

Membership Committee—This committee gets you involved and interacting with potential new members as well as current members. It's a terrific committee to be involved with for easy introductions and networking.

Program/Speaker Committee—This committee identifies and approaches industry leaders to speak at association events. Being involved with this committee is a great way to get connected to thought-leaders in your industry. It also improves your influence in the industry by being known by these movers and shakers, not to mention your ability to name-drop by knowing them (persuasion principle of social proof).

Finally, being a member of a professional association gives you access to the membership directory. This directory can be easily used to identify professionals in your industry for networking (as well as identifying companies for any marketing purposes). Properly handled, your membership in an association will frequently, though not always, gain you a brief networking conversation with another member.

The more deeply connected you are (or can become) in professional associations, the greater your chances of tapping into the Hidden Job Market and shortening your job search.

Association/Industry Conferences

Association and industry conferences are great events for job-search networking. They present an opportunity to meet face-to-face with industry colleagues and hiring executives. You can learn which companies are potentially hiring. Occasionally you can get insider information on companies of interest to you. If you are a seasoned professional who has attended professional conferences, you know there is as much covert recruiting and informal interviewing taking place as actual business interaction with potential clients and customers.

Conferences can be expensive (not just the registration fee, but also travel and lodging). However, attending and investing in one major industry conference is a good job-search strategy.

Discover whether the sponsoring organization has local chapters. Some do, and they frequently hold regular monthly or quarterly meetings. Local chapter meetings tend to be breakfast or after-hours meetings. The cost for these local meetings is usually little or nothing, if you are a member of the organization. Attend as many as possible and build your network.

Use the following strategies to get the most out of attending a professional conference and further your job search:

1. Do research using lists of attendees and exhibitors. Every industry conference requires you to register. Registrants often get advance notice listing the attendees and exhibitors (potential employers). Look at both lists for any hiring executives who will attend. This is invaluable information for you. Make it a goal to meet and speak with them. Research the executives on LinkedIn, and see if you have anyone in common who can introduce you via email or LinkedIn before the conference.

Research the companies who will be at the conference as well. Too many job seekers come to conferences unprepared. Your research will edge out your competition. Check out each company online, as well as their jobs page, if one exists. See if they are looking to hire someone with your skills and background. Also, find out from the conference materials when the exhibit hall is open. You'll probably do most of your job-search networking while other potential job seekers are aimlessly wandering the booths.

2. Come prepared with your elevator speech, resume, and business cards. Be ready to use your elevator speech. Bring plenty of resumes, but only offer one if asked. Put each resume in an envelope with your name on it so it can be transported easily (and discreetly) in a suit or portfolio. Business cards are a must, especially for circumstances that don't allow for an extended discussion about employment. Make the contact, have a good conversation, and exchange business cards. You can communicate more fully later and supply a resume (if appropriate). Make sure you put a short note on the back of each business card you receive so that you can remember something about the person or your conversation with them. This is a lifesaver when following up later.

3. Keep your attire conservative and employ a solid conference game plan. First impressions are critical, so conservative business attire is a requirement. Overdressed is better than underdressed. Dressing in conservative attire portrays professionalism and taps into the persuasion principle of authority. Survey the layout of the conference before you arrive (using the conference materials). Map out the companies that interest you and put them in order of your personal preference, high interest to low interest. Keep in mind that your order may have to change if a lower-priority company has a booth very close to a higher-priority one. As a matter of convenience, you may drop in on a lower-priority company before the higher-priority one. When you arrive at the conference, see if any new companies registered too late to be included in your materials, and see if any of them need to be included on your "company hit list." If you see someone you know at a conference, saying hello is fine, but clinging to them is not.[114] You're there to expand your network and connect to your next job, not waste precious time socializing.

4. Remember: Every conversation is an interview. Use your elevator speech and remember the three keys to kicking off a good interview or conversation: make eye contact, offer a firm handshake, and show enthusiasm. Be prepared with a few questions for the person you are

---

114 Weiss, Tara. "Find Your Job by Going to a Conference," *Forbes*, March 24, 2009, http://www.forbes.com/2009/03/24/conference-job-seeking-leadership-careers-networking.html (accessed July 10, 2015).

speaking with. If in doubt, "What do you think of the [conference] so far?"[115] works well. (More on this in a moment.)

You are most likely being interviewed from the moment you speak with a company representative or hiring executive, but don't bring up the topic of open positions right away. That may make things awkward. Read the situation before asking. Most people will understand your ultimate goal and will offer help, either at the conference or during post-conference communication.

5. Following up is crucial to your success. You'll likely use email to do this, and contacting every relevant connection you made at the conference may take a lot of time. But you never know which connection will lead to your next job. Use all of the business cards you collected and create a brief follow-up email (or LinkedIn InMail) to each (which is where the notes you recorded on the back of each card pay dividends).

The idea of walking into a conference filled with strangers can be intimidating. That's completely understandable and you are not alone in that feeling. However, networking is very important to your job search. Follow the steps in this section. Research. Plan your strategy. Bring your business cards and practice your elevator speech. And then meet people. After the first few, initiating conversations will get easier (and you won't be able to wait to talk to the next person!).

Icebreaker Questions for Conferences and Events

Often the most intimidating part about networking at a conference or event is starting a conversation. After an introduction, it's uncomfortable to deal with that awkward moment of silence. The trick to overcoming that awkwardness is to be prepared with a handful of conversation starters—icebreaker questions.

When engaging in a conversation, be present and focus. Use

---

115 Ibid.

open-ended questions starting with "what" and "how" whenever possible. Start all networking conversations with the idea of creating a "conversation surplus" for the other person. Let them fill the "conversation bucket" about them. Be a good, interested listener. Only speak of yourself when they ask. Otherwise, keep the focus on them. Let them create the surplus in the conversation.

More often than not, a networking conversation balances out and ends up being equal in terms of the sharing of information and time spent in conversation.

If the conversation ends with a significant surplus in your fellow attendee's favor, that's fine. Praise yourself for being a good listener. You don't know how that seemingly lopsided conversation might benefit you in the future.

Here are some good icebreaker questions to spur conversation:

- What do you do? (Follow up with a request for their opinion on an industry issue, trend, event, or something else)
- What motivated you to come to this conference/event?
- What do you think of the lineup of speakers?
- What did you think of the last speaker?
- What are you finding most interesting (or valuable) about this conference?
- Attendance looks good. Do you come every year?
- What's keeping you (or your company) busy these days?

Once the conversation begins and the initial discomfort dissipates, an engaging conversation can start to develop. As a good networker, always offer to help a contact whenever you can with the understanding that they will do what they can to help you. Remember, in networking, "those who give . . . get."[116]

---

116 Vlooten, "The Seven Laws."

Goals for Attending a Conference or Networking Event

Before you attend a conference or any networking event, it is important to prioritize your goals for why you are attending. Here is a list to help you:

1. **Meet new people**—Make it a point to meet as many new contacts as possible. Specifically, you want to meet and engage all targeted contacts who have the potential to move your job search forward.

2. **Enhance existing relationships**—Nurture and maintain the relationships you have with existing connections. Deepen the relationship and find ways to support each other.

3. **Learn**—Listen carefully and learn from every conversation. Record pertinent information on the back of a business card or in a notepad after the engagement. Be in the moment and you will be surprised what you might learn that could advance your job search.

4. **Enjoy yourself**—Have some fun! Socialize. However, be conscious of what you are doing and how you are using your time. Time at networking events is precious. Use it wisely.[117]

This next statement goes without saying, but here it is anyway: Never ask a contact for a job at an event! It will significantly dilute the engagement. Instead, do all the right networking things, then when appropriate, ask for help in spreading the word, seek advice, but don't ask for a job.[118]

A Few Points of Etiquette When Networking at an Event

In the hustle and bustle of an event, there can be a lot of things to

---

117 Phillips, *Guide to Professional Networking*, p. 50–51.
118 See also, Leibman, "9 Keys."

remember and think about. Here's a quick review of networking behaviors that will make the most impact:

Don't ask for a job. Many job seekers fail to grasp the significance of this. Asking for a job creates an awkward moment and will derail an otherwise good networking conversation. Don't do it.

Don't stretch a conversation. Recognize when the conversation has run its course or the contact wants to conclude the engagement.

Be present. Avoid scanning the room when in a conversation. Focus on your contact and the content of the conversation.

Listen and engage. Listen and ask open-ended questions. Engage in conversation and probe. You will be surprised what you learn and from whom.

Being aware of these points of etiquette will create a better first impression of you as a professional (or improve the impression others may already have). They will be more likely to help you in your job search.

Alumni Groups

There are a variety of alumni organizations. These include colleges and universities, fraternities and sororities, academic associations, company alumni groups, and others. Alumni directories and LinkedIn groups can be rich resources for contacts.

More LinkedIn alumni groups are posting jobs, job leads, and discussions as a way to create interaction and activity within their membership. It's a way to create value for their members. Joining an alumni group could lead you to a hidden or little-known job opening.

When reaching out to an alumnus, treat the contact like any other networking contact. The advantage you have is you have something in common to immediately reference. When tapping into an alumni network, follow these guidelines:

- Identify alumni who would be a good fit for your needs . . .

someone who might be in a position to assist you. If you are an engineer, an alumnus who is a psychiatrist may not have the career or networking correlation you're looking for. Identify fit-for-purpose alums.

- Connect and engage by asking for information, just as you would with any other networking contact.
- Only suggest or ask for an introduction to others in their network after you have established rapport or a level of trust. This could be during a second or third engagement. Don't push.
- And don't ask for a job.

Alumni groups can be a good source for networking and job leads. The presumption is these alums will be more likely to help you as a result of your shared background and experience.

Referring and Connecting

A very persuasive technique to differentiate yourself from other job seekers, (it's a powerful technique in business and life, too) is to connect others for their mutual benefit. You can clearly set yourself apart by referring a high-caliber, high-value contact to a networking contact or hiring executive.

To be effective in a job search, you must use this technique in a well-timed and deftly executed manner. The referral must be for something meaningful or significant.[119] It must have value. And you must be reasonably sure that it will be well received. If you're not sure, it may be best to pass on using this approach.

Here's an example of how this scenario might work: In the course of a networking conversation, you learn that your networking contact is looking to hire a new accounting firm. You just so happen

---

119 Coburn, Derek. *Networking Is Not Working: Stop Collecting Business Cards and Start Making Meaningful Connections.* (Idea Press Publishing, 2014), p. 52–59.

to personally know one of the city's best accountants, and his firm is top-notch. He is experienced, credentialed . . . it's a nice fit. How can you use this discovery to your advantage?

First, you have a choice to make on timing. Depending upon how the conversation or engagement is unfolding and the level of rapport, you can immediately let the networking contact know that you have a connection to a very well-qualified accountant who you would be delighted to connect him/her with. Or you may choose to wait, thereby not diverting the conversation into a tangent topic. You can mention your accountant friend later or by email after the engagement. Or you may choose to do nothing at all with the information. The choice is yours depending upon your professional judgment.

Any referral you do make must be to someone you have very high confidence in. This cannot be overstated. Your referral is a reflection on you as a professional. Never refer someone you do not know or do not have full confidence in.[120] Doing so can backfire and damage your reputation. In the accountant scenario, your contact is not only a CPA, but a lawyer (JD) with an advanced LLM[121] degree in taxation and a nice guy. Someone you can refer with confidence!

Like any networking conversation, any referral you offer must be done without expecting anything in return—even though you hope the gesture earns you a few points. However, be aware that by freely providing a referral, you will tap into the persuasion principles of:

- Authority (you're connected—a center of influence)

- Social proof (based on what your contact will say about you)

- Reciprocity (the need to return the favor . . . with a job offer, maybe?)

And, of course, your referral (the accountant) will appreciate the

---

120 Ibid., p. 40.

121 "Master of laws," usually targeted to a specific discipline; see "What Is an LLM?" LLM Guide, http://www.llm-guide.com/what-is-an-llm (accessed November 10, 2015).

connection and will look for opportunities to assist you in your job search, now or later.

Face-to-Face Networking as an Introvert

Networking can be more challenging if you are introverted. Meeting new people face-to-face just does not come as easy to you as it does for others. Fortunately, there are some very practical strategies you can use to defuse much of the anxiety of networking. They are:

- Remind yourself of the value networking has to your job search. Sixty to eighty percent of all jobs are a result of some form of networking.[122] Psych yourself up the best you can (without alcohol!).

- Go to smaller events. Avoid conferences or association events that are attended by the thousands and look for opportunities where the attendees are more in the hundreds, instead.[123]

- Focus on groups where you have a common interest or common purpose. For example, if you're a nurse in workers' compensation, look for a group comprised of nurse case managers. Conversation will be easier because you have knowledge of and interest in the topics of conversation. These types of functions often have educational sessions, which gives you a reason for being there if you feel the need to state one.

- Before attending a function, create a list of three or four icebreaker questions. Use the previous section on icebreaker questions as a guide. Preparation is key. At an event with unfamiliar people, you may become distracted by your surroundings and forget a few things—having your list of

---

122 LinkedIn, "Using LinkedIn to Find a Job"; Beatty, "The Math Behind the Networking Claim"; Rothberg, "80% of Job Openings."

123 Townsend, Maya. "The Introvert's Survival Guide to Networking," Inc.com, http://www.inc.com/maya-townsend/introvert-networking-guide.html (accessed November 4, 2015).

questions will make conversations with other attendees much easier.

- Finally, know how to close a conversation. When the conversation has run its course and the silence begins to feel awkward, have a closing line that will politely allow you to move on. For example, "It has been a pleasure speaking with you. I'm sure you have others to meet as do I. Do you have a card?"

Social psychologist Amy Cuddy has a TED Talk that discusses "power posing"—standing in a posture of confidence—and its positive results in interviewing (the concepts work equally for any networking event). The talk begins with the science then shifts the findings to practical application for interviews (and networking). It will help anyone hesitant about engaging in networking.[124] When properly done, networking will open doors to opportunities. To be a successful networker, give far more than you ever expect to receive. Over time, you will discover that you have received more than you gave.

Your Network: At the End of Your Job Search

When you land your next career opportunity, announce it to your network. You especially want to inform those who were more integral to the success of your search.

It's a nice touch in these communications to indicate who you are working for, what your new role is, and why you are excited about the opportunity. In many cases, you'll get some well-wishes for future success, which will feel good.

Even though your job search is complete, continue to stay in touch with your network. Don't disappear! And be a professional networker and always offer and be willing to help.

---

124 Cuddy, Amy. "Your Body Language Shapes Who You Are." TEDGlobal video, 21:02. Filmed June 2012. http://www.ted.com/talks/amy_cuddy_your_body_language_shapes_who_you_are?language=en (accessed March 17, 2016).

PART III

Networking with Recruiters

Just begin and the mind grows heated; continue,
and the task will be completed!
— Goethe[125]

According to surveys conducted by the American Staffing Association, over 90 percent of employers have or would use an executive recruiter to fill open positions.[126] This section will cover how to find

125 "Johann Wolfgang von Goethe Quotable Quote," Goodreads, http://www.goodreads.com/quotes/316359-just-begin-and-the-mind-grows-heated-continue-and-the (accessed June 11, 2015).

126 DISYS, "Top 5 Reasons to Use Staffing Firms as Your Primary Hiring Strategy," http://www.disys.com/top-5-reasons-to-use-staffing-firms-as-your-primary-hiring-strategy/ (accessed June 19, 2015); "Get Help With Hiring . . . And More: Working With Staffing Firms: What's in It for Me?" CareerBuilder, http://www.careerbuildercommunications.com/staffing-firms/ (accessed June 19, 2015).

recruiters who fit your industry or position and how to work with them effectively to enhance your search.[127]

What Recruiters Can and Cannot Do for You

Recruiters can be a terrific resource during a job search. They should not be your leading source for landing your next job, simply because they are hired and paid by clients to find well-qualified candidates, not find jobs for job seekers.[128] That being said, the search and placement business is a billion dollar industry,[129] and job seekers get identified and placed by recruiters every day. In fact, networking with recruiters can lead you to open positions that other job seekers will never know about. According to a survey conducted by LinkedIn, only 18 percent of job seekers think of search firms when looking for a new job.[130] Recruiters are not "top of mind." This creates an opportunity for you. By identifying and contacting executive recruiters, you are tapping into a channel of potential opportunities that most job seekers neglect. The trick is to be found and have the right qualifications at the right time. Here is a non-exhaustive list of benefits of aligning yourself with a recruiter:

1. They can introduce you to job opportunities with their clients.

2. They often have insight on opportunities with their clients before they are made public.

3. They can help you determine your market value.

---

127 See also, Claycomb and Dinse, *Career Pathways*, Part 6.

128 "Don't Do That!—Mistakes To Avoid When Working With Recruiters," True Source (blog), November 2012, http://www.true-source.com/2012/11/dont-do-that-mistakes-to-avoid-when-working-with-recruiters/ (accessed June 9, 2015).

129 "Employment and Recruiting Agencies in the US: Market Research Report," IBISWorld, March 2015, http://www.ibisworld.com/industry/default.aspx?indid=1463 (accessed June 11, 2015).

130 LinkedIn Talent Solutions. "2015 Talent Trends: Insights for Research and Staffing Recruiters on What Talent Wants Around the World," p. 17, https://business.linkedin.com/content/dam/business/talent-solutions/global/en_us/c/pdfs/global-talent-trends-staff-report.pdf (accessed November 23, 2015).

4. They frequently can provide you with much more information about the position, company, and culture than what you can discover on your own.

5. They can prepare you for interviews and inform you about hot buttons to hit upon and landmines to avoid.

6. They can give advice on how to manage the interview process, often because they are a consultant on the types and timing of communications with the employer.

7. They can provide insight and advice during offer negotiations.

8. They can counsel you through the resignation process (should that apply to you).

There are also things that a recruiter cannot or will not do for you:

1. Hold your hand and become your nursemaid during your job search.

2. Get you a job. Remember, recruiters are hired to find qualified candidates for their clients, not find you a job.

3. Unless you become a viable candidate in an active search with the recruiter, they will not spend an inordinate amount of time with you discussing your resume, the job market, interview strategy, and other free advice.

The key to working with recruiters is knowing what to expect from them and controlling your own expectations. Recruiters can be a valued resource, but the responsibility for your search lies with you and your efforts.

Retainer and Contingency Search Firms

Before we discuss how to target and contact recruiters, it's beneficial to have a basic understanding of the two types of search firms you'll likely encounter as a professional-level job seeker: retainer and contingency. We'll briefly describe the differences then move on to how to engage and work with them.

If a firm works on a retained basis, they are generally paid an upfront fee to begin search activities. Then, at certain predetermined points along the search timeline, the firm is paid another installment. Final payment is usually made upon completion of the search assignment.[131] Fully retained searches are generally used for senior executive and C-level positions with larger organizations.

A contingency firm is paid differently. As the name implies, their fee is contingent and is earned only when a referred candidate is hired by a client. It is strictly pay-for-performance.[132]

It used to be said that contingency firms are paid for performance while retainer firms are paid for process, regardless of whether the position gets filled. In large measure, it is this "pay for performance rather than process" that has led to the continued growth of the recruiting industry's contingency side. In fact, many retainer firms now conduct contingency searches to compete for the revenue flow of clients who prefer a contingency arrangement. Contingency firms also conduct retainer searches and function in similar ways, with the same (and sometimes more) resources, blurring the distinction between the two types. What this means for you as a job seeker, is that it doesn't matter how the firm is paid. What does matter is whether the firm can match you to an open position with one of its clients.

---

131 Hallowell, Kirk. *The Million Dollar Race: An Insider's Guide to Winning Your Dream Job.* (Austin, TX: Greenleaf Book Group Press, 2013), p. 112.

132 Ibid., p. 111.

Contract or Project Firms

Both of these types of firms are prevalent in the technology field. These firms lease the employee to a company for long periods of time (occasionally up to and over a year). Generally speaking, these assignments are paid on an hourly basis or on a contract arrangement. These contract positions can result in permanent employment or a renewal of the project employment contract.

How to Find Recruiters

Identifying and contacting recruiters is not as difficult as you might think. Below are three effective methods. We recommend that you use all three. They are:

1. Calling hiring executives in your industry.

2. Calling colleagues in your industry.

3. Researching recruiters online (most notably, using LinkedIn).

Let's discuss these approaches in detail.

Calling Hiring Executives

One of the best methods for identifying recruiters is to reach out to hiring executives and ask for referrals. Think about it: Who better at identifying and referring you to potential recruiters than the executives who hire them, right?

This method has three major advantages. First, it is an easy call to make. You are asking for help, and most people will help you if they can. Asking for referrals to recruiters is a safe and reasonable topic for your call.

Second, this method will lead you to the industry's top recruiters. Connecting with them will expand your reach for potential opportunities.

Finally, and most importantly, you will be speaking with hiring executives who could have an opportunity, such as described in the "Hidden Job Market," or know of one in the industry. Hint: It's extremely helpful here to be ready with your elevator speech.

How do you go about calling these hiring executives? Here are the steps:

1. Identify companies that interest you.

2. Research and determine who the likely hiring executive is for the position you would be interested in.

3. Pick up the phone and make a call. Engage the hiring executive in a conversation, explain your situation, and as part of the conversation, ask whether he/she could identify and pass along to you the names of a few recruiters.

This technique is effective because job seekers call the hiring executive. The ultimate goal is to speak to the executive and have a voice-to-voice conversation. Avoid using email as it dilutes this technique's effectiveness.

Because this technique is such a powerful way to network with hiring executives, here is a script you can use or modify:

Introduction:
"[First name of the hiring executive or Mr./Ms.], this is (state your name). I'm a clinical nurse manager with thirteen years' experience in the population health management industry. I am looking to make a career move, and I would like your advice and assistance regarding my search."

Confirm you have the right contact:
"If I have it right, you are the hiring executive (or use the executive's title) for case and nurse managers. Here's what I'm looking for . . . I am looking for the names of recruiters I can contact who specialize in (title of your position). I am hoping that you could refer me to a few recruiters you like."

Assume the hiring executive will help:
"Do you know of any recruiters you feel good about? Maybe some good ones you've used in the past?"

Show appreciation and (maybe) ask one question:
"Thank you. Let me ask you since I have you on the phone: What do you think the effects of healthcare reform will be on the population health management industry?"

If you're unemployed, close and offer to send your resume:
"Again, thank you. I appreciate your help. If it's okay, I'm going to email my resume to you just so you have it. Feel free to forward it to others as you deem appropriate."

For anyone who helps you, send a thank-you email. Depending upon the conversation, it could be appropriate to send a LinkedIn invitation.

There are a couple of reasons why calling hiring executives for referrals to recruiters is a powerful technique. First and foremost, it gets you talking with hiring executives, which could lead to a job opening with that company! Second, hiring executives are the people who typically approve the payment of recruiting fees. Therefore, when you call a recruiter later saying you were referred by one of their paying clients, that will help get their attention, and they should take or quickly return your call. The recruiter does not want to say that they did not speak with you if the hiring executive asks later.

When properly executed, this approach will get you several names of recruiters who likely specialize in your industry or position type. If you hear the same names being held in high regard, you've likely discovered your industry's best recruiters—and, in the process, possibly some to avoid.

Most importantly, you have connected with hiring executives in the industry. Those contacts can pay big dividends in your career in the short or long term.

Calling Your Colleagues in the Industry

The advantages of contacting your own industry colleagues are many. You can have open and frank discussions regarding recruiters. You will be able to create a list of several recruiters who call your colleagues. You might learn about a few recruiters whom you may elect not to contact. And, networking with colleagues may result in job leads.

These calls are easy to make. The hazard is you can easily get tied up in long conversations that eat up your time and distract you from your real goal of getting a new job.

Researching LinkedIn and the Internet

Search LinkedIn for recruiters. By using the keyword feature, you may limit your search to recruiters with a specialty that matches your background, experience, or interests. Search your LinkedIn groups for recruiters.

Another fast way to obtain names of your industry's recruiters is to search the Internet. There are online services that maintain nationwide databases of recruiters. One particular website and organization where you can describe a recruiter by industry and location, and find one to match your profile, is http://www.mrinetwork.com.

Another way to compile a list of recruiters tailored to your industry is to search through the Directory of Executive Recruiters (Kennedy Publications). Updated annually, this publication is classified by geography and specialty.

For local searches, the local business journals frequently include in their Book of Lists names of search firms. The firms are listed by the number of recruiters and the specialties that the firm works with.

Contacting a Recruiter

If your first contact with a recruiter is by email, keep it short but impactful. Identify your role or function (title) and highlight a couple of accomplishments. Do not send a lengthy email! Recruiters are time sensitive, and the mere appearance of a long email will dissuade them from reading it. Attach a copy of your resume. Ask for a call, but follow up with the recruiter in a couple of days if you have not heard back.

If your first contact with a recruiter is a proactive call, start your conversation by getting their attention. Begin your conversation (or voice message) with an attention-getting statement. The most impactful approach is to name the person who referred you, if you have one. Another way would be to mention an accomplishment: "Bob, my name is Linda, and I am an award-winning marketing professional with seventeen years of experience in the commercial real estate industry. I am exploring a career move, and I would like to discuss how we might be able to work together."

Stay in routine contact with the recruiters you feel can help you. This can be done with a call or email. Most all recruiters will permit this kind of routine communication. The key here is to keep your name in front of the recruiter, not to be a pest. Turning off a recruiter is closing a door to a potential opportunity. It's a fine line that really turns on the level of position you are seeking. Contacting a recruiter once only every three or four weeks is adequate.

Finding a Recruiter Who Can Help You

When talking with recruiters, ask questions. The following questions can help you decide whether the recruiter is a good match for you, now or in the future:

1. In what industry do you do most of your work?

2. What types of positions do you fill?

3. Based on my background, am I a viable candidate for you?

4. (If you fit within the recruiter's specialty) Can I send you a LinkedIn invitation?

When there is not a match with the recruiter's specialty

If the recruiter tells you they can't be of assistance, ask for the names of any other recruiters they may know who can help you. If they don't know of anyone, do not be disappointed. They may not have contacts who specialize in your area of interest. You could also ask the recruiter for general assistance, but be sensitive to the recruiter's time! Here are a couple of questions you could ask:

1. What is your opinion of the job market?

2. If you were in my shoes, what would you be doing to advance your job search?

When there's a match between your background and the recruiter's specialty

If there is a match between your background and the recruiter's specialty, provide and volunteer any information requested by the recruiter, especially a resume if you have not already provided one.

Even if there is a match between your background and the recruiter, understand that most of the time, they will not be able to help you immediately. This is simply a function of timing. They may not have an active assignment that fits your background, geographic location, or other factors. Just because they cannot place you today does not mean that they cannot place you in the future.

When a Recruiter Finds and Contacts You

Recruiters contact job seekers either by phone or email (specifically through LinkedIn InMail). Make sure your personal email is synced with LinkedIn so when a recruiter contacts you through LinkedIn you receive the email immediately.

When a recruiter contacts you, be flattered. There is a high likelihood that you have been referred or your career background and achievements have caught the eye of the recruiter. You might be a fit for a currently open position. Respond promptly. Evaluation begins with the timeliness of your response.

If the recruiter contacts you by phone and the timing of the call is not good, ask to return the call . . . and definitely do so! Recruiters fully understand that their calls can catch you "out of the blue." Ask to call back or schedule an appointment.

Be appreciative. Regardless of your interest in the position, always show appreciation to the recruiter. Contact from a recruiter is a channel for opportunity that you want to nurture and have available to you.

When you speak with the recruiter, be present. Resist the temptation to multitask during the conversation. Treat the conversation like you would a telephone interview with a hiring executive.

Ask questions. The dialogue should be an exchange of information. Learn about the opportunity, the company, job requirements, why the position is open, as well as compensation and its range (this is fine for an initial conversation). You and the recruiter should jointly determine whether you are a good match for the position. If so, great! If not, say so. There's no reason to pursue an opportunity you are not qualified for or interested in.

Do not "Decline" a LinkedIn message from a recruiter. When you do, it creates a record that the recruiter will see the next time the recruiter has another opportunity. Any record of a "Decline" could motivate the recruiter to bypass you and contact others. Instead, if you are not interested in an opportunity at a particular time for any of a variety of reasons, simply thank the recruiter for thinking of you. That response is polite and keeps the door open for the future.

How to Successfully Work with a Recruiter: Some Recruiter Etiquette Dos and Don'ts

To cultivate a positive working relationship with a recruiter now or in the future, here are several key items to know:

1. Never lie or stretch the truth about your experience, education, income, or anything else about your background. Recruiters are uncanny in eventually discovering the truth, and when they do, you're finished.

2. Never go around a recruiter and approach an employer about an opportunity that the recruiter informed you about (without permission). If you do, you will be forever banished from the recruiter's contact list.

3. Offer to open your connections and LinkedIn contacts for the recruiter's use. The recruiter will appreciate the offer.

4. Acknowledge and return calls promptly. Recruiters almost always have a reason for calling. Get back to them as soon as you reasonably can.

5. If you are not interested in a particular opportunity, try to refer the recruiter to someone who would be qualified.

6. If you get involved in interviewing for an opening and decide the opportunity is not for you, tell the recruiter promptly and exit the process. Again, try to refer the recruiter to others who might be qualified.

7. Do not use a recruiter to get an offer just to elicit a counteroffer from your current employer. Taking a counteroffer is a shortsighted career move, and you will alienate the recruiter from contacting you again if you accept the counteroffer.

Recruiters can be a rich resource for your job search and the industry you work in. Foster good relationships with recruiters. Developing a relationship with a recruiter is priceless. Recruiters have long memories. Helping a recruiter can benefit your career greatly in both the short and long term.

Some final advice regarding recruiters

- Remember, recruiters work for the employer, not you. They will call you if and when they have a potential opportunity that fits your qualifications.
- Connect with recruiters who specialize in your industry or position type, preferably both.
- Stay in touch with recruiters, just don't become a pest.
- Always return a recruiter's call promptly.
- Always give referrals—ask if you can help the recruiter.

Networking with the right recruiters and connecting with them can be an effective channel to appropriate job opportunities and job-search advice.

PART IV

Social Media and Networking: Twitter and Facebook

*There is in this world no such force as the
force of a man determined to rise.*
— W. E. B. DuBois[133]

Social media has drastically changed how you network and conduct a job search. The big three online professional/social sites are: LinkedIn, Twitter, and Facebook.

We have already discussed LinkedIn. It is clearly the most prevalent online professional networking site. We will now explore

---

133 Pine, Joslyn. Ed., *Book of African-American Quotations*. (New York: Dover Publications, 2011), p. 51.

using Twitter and Facebook as components of networking and your job search.

Twitter

Twitter has quickly become part of the arsenal used by employers and recruiters to reach qualified job seekers. According to a recent survey by Jobvite, for the first time more than half (52 percent) of recruiters are using Twitter for talent search.[134] Getting dialed into Twitter can help you in your job search. The percentage of job seekers using Twitter continues to increase year after year. In 2011, 26 percent of job seekers used Twitter, which increased to 34 percent in 2012.[135] This is likely due to its increasing effectiveness and its use by younger generations who grew up with the technology. In fact, research shows that 23 percent of Internet users surveyed, age eighteen or over, used Twitter in 2014, with an increase in every age bracket.[136]

One very unique feature about Twitter that enhances its job-search value is that you can follow anyone you wish, including companies, target contacts, thought-leaders, HR and corporate recruiters, and more without requesting permission (unlike LinkedIn and Facebook). This openness can be a profound resource for information, identifying job leads, job opportunities, and communicating with those who can help you and hire you.

If you are new to Twitter, here are some pointers to get you started:

Create Your Twitter Username (Handle). This is nothing more than a name that appears as you tweet (slang for posting a message). You're

---

134 "2014 Social Recruiting Survey," Jobvite, https://www.jobvite.com/wp-content/uploads/2014/10/Jobvite_SocialRecruiting_Survey2014.pdf (accessed June 1, 2015).

135 Adams, Susan. "4 Ways to Use Twitter to Find a Job," *Forbes*, November 30, 2012, http://www.forbes.com/sites/susanadams/2012/11/30/4-ways-to-use-twitter-to-find-a-job/ (accessed June 16, 2015).

136 Duggan, Maeve, Nicole B. Ellison, Cliff Lampe, Amanda Lenhart, and Mary Madden, "Demographics of Key Social Networking Platforms," Pew Research Center, January 9, 2015, http://www.pewinternet.org/2015/01/09/demographics-of-key-social-networking-platforms-2/ (accessed June 16, 2015).

permitted fifteen characters for a name or handle. You can use your own name, nickname, or any other descriptive name—so long as it is professional.

Set up Your Twitter Profile. Your profile is limited to 160 characters including spaces. So you must be succinct but impactful with your description. Review your elevator speech, branding message, and network/resume business cards. Then formulate your professional profile. Explore other Twitter profiles for ideas if needed.

Add a photo, likely the same as the one that appears on your LinkedIn profile. Since your Twitter profile is so short, add a link to other sites, most notably LinkedIn.

Here are a couple partial profiles to get you thinking:

Award-winning care management sales professional . . .

Seasoned operational management executive . . .

Once you have an account, establish a handle, and write a profile, you are ready to go!

Now that you're set up, here are some steps to use Twitter in your job search:

Create a second account if necessary, then follow target companies and people. For job seekers with established personal Twitter accounts, it's recommended to create a second one solely for your job search. Identify and begin following target companies of interest to you. This can be an edge over other job seekers, as well as a great source of information to further your search since most major or established organizations have a corporate Twitter account. A growing trend is using Twitter first to announce open positions.[137] Following industry thought leaders, hiring executives, human resource professionals, recruiters, and so on can help as well. To help you identify employers and people to follow, check out: http://www.twellow.com.

---

137 Dickler, Jessica. "Get Your Holiday Job—on Twitter!" CNNMoney, October 21, 2010, http://money.cnn.com/2010/10/21/pf/job_openings_on_twitter/ (accessed June 4, 2015).

Use hashtags well. Twitter uses hashtags (the # symbol) as an index or filing system of sorts. It's a way to search Twitter for topics or specific information. You can use this indexing system to look for job leads. Below is a short list of hashtags that can help lead you to possible job openings:

#jobs
#jobsearch
#employment
#resume
#careers
#nowhiring

Think creatively about how to use hashtags and you may discover hidden openings.

You can use the hashtag indexing system to narrow your search by location or function. For example:

"#Dallas" + "#jobs"—jobs in Dallas
"#jobs" + "#sales"—jobs in sales
"#jobs" + "#accounting" + "#omaha"—accounting jobs in Omaha

Use Twitter job search engines. Use job search engines such as TwitJobSearch (http://twitter.com/twitjobsearch), Jobcritters (https://www.jobcritters.com), and Careerarc (https://www.careerarc.com) to stay well informed and up to date on the latest job postings from target companies and search firms.

These sites allow job seekers to choose from over six thousand job categories and then be notified when a job fits chosen parameters. It's similar to receiving an Indeed.com or LinkedIn job alert.

Create content. When you create a tweet, Twitter only gives you 140 characters, including spaces and a link. You must be brief and to the point with your messages.

You can tweet and retweet (forwarding someone else's posted

message) as much as you like (just don't overdo it). The key is to create interesting and relevant content. This can be tricky, so abbreviating words in your tweets is acceptable and necessary. Share news, links, and professional insight. Respond to others' shares and answer questions. The most important thing is to think before you post. As a professional job seeker, your tweets reflect directly on you. Others form an opinion and an impression of you based on what you post and how you express it.

Overall, Twitter's use and acceptance can be industry specific. In other words, some industries may use it more than others. Regardless, Twitter is gaining wider acceptance by employers and recruiters every year. Twitter is a job search tool that should be seriously considered and used as part of your strategy, but its impact will rely on your use and your industry's acceptance and use of it.

Facebook

When it comes to Facebook, the lines between social and professional networking have blurred. Facebook has historically been viewed as a purely social networking venue for "kids." That has changed. As younger professionals enter the job market and advance their careers, many have repurposed Facebook into a professional networking tool, with a personal touch. In fact, many job seekers view Facebook as a job search tool that showcases the "whole person," not just the professional.

Companies have caught on. Most larger, established, and forward-thinking companies now have a corporate Facebook presence. They use Facebook to attract job seekers and to check an applicant's background and character.

As a job search tool, Facebook is similar to LinkedIn. You will discover similarities as we discuss Facebook. Some of these points will be shorter because concepts have already been more thoroughly covered in the LinkedIn section. Similarities include:

Profile. Like LinkedIn and Twitter, you need to create a professional Facebook profile. It appears under the "Timeline" heading. Align your Facebook and LinkedIn profiles.

If you already have a Facebook account and you have been using it socially with your friends, it's time to get out the mop and bucket and clean it up! Remove all unprofessional posts. Remove all unprofessional or suspect photos. From this point forward, all posts and photos must be acceptable to the professional viewing audience (hiring executives, corporate HR, executive recruiters, and so on).

Similar to LinkedIn, use keywords and industry terms-of-art to enhance your "find-ability." Consider linking to or mentioning your LinkedIn profile. Make sure they are consistent with employment, dates, and so on.

Classify your friends. This is similar to tagging your connections on LinkedIn. Go to your friends list and put the cursor over the rectangle next to each name. From there you can create a "New List." Create a list for your professional friends/contacts. The benefit of this is you can later post information directed only to your professional contacts. As you add professional friends, classify them to this list. Depending on the number of friends you have, it could take you a while to do this, but it is worth it. Be sure that any professional contacts you add are relevant to you.

"Like" and follow target company pages and search firms. By doing this, you will receive information about job openings, announcements, news releases, and so on. This is very similar to following a company on LinkedIn.

Use Facebook to do more than follow. You can search within Facebook on a wide variety of topics (likes, interests, groups, and so on), like a search engine inside Facebook.

Post relevant content. Similar to Twitter and LinkedIn, post relevant content and pass along good information as it comes your way. Remember to think and be smart about what you post.

Protect Your Facebook Privacy. To ensure what you are sharing with the public and potential employers during a search is appropriate, convert any post that is either Public or visible to Friends of Friends into strictly Friends Only posts. To create Friends Only posts, at the top of your Facebook page, choose settings, then select Privacy from the left menu. Under the "Who can see my stuff?" section, click "Limit the Audience" for posts shared with Friends of Friends or Public. Facebook will then warn you that, even though you may change your posts to Friends Only, they'll still be visible to friends of anyone tagged. Continue by clicking on "Limit Old Posts."

One final thing, make sure all your future posts are still set to Friends Only. Always keep in mind anything you post online is a good representation of yourself, and consider your job search audience being able to find it.

Some final words on Facebook. Traditionally viewed as a purely social site, Facebook is now a significant resource tool for a job search. Will Facebook ever surpass LinkedIn as a professional networking site? Who's to say? It's certain Facebook is another tool that today's job seeker can use to advance and shorten a job search.

A Caution about Online Networking

Online networking is a powerful job-search strategy and tool. Properly used, it can and will advance your job search. It can also be a tremendous time-waster! It is very easy to get caught up, clicking away and connecting with others who have only a remote chance of advancing your job search, but "you never know." Or you can end up having delightful online communications that make you feel good— which is okay—but really do not serve any job-search purpose, but "you never know," right? Wrong.

Be careful! Before you know it, two hours of your precious time can be gone and your search hasn't budged one inch. The advice here is simple: Be aware of the purpose of what you are doing and the amount of time you are spending on online professional and social media sites. If you catch yourself asking whether your activities on online networking sites are advancing your job search, you've likely crossed the line into busywork.

What Employers Find on Social Media

As discussed, it is undeniable that social media will play a role in your job search. The significance of that role depends largely on how much you use social media. But your networking contacts and employers also use social media.

A Society for Human Resource Management survey found that 52 percent of employers use social networks to screen potential job candidates (this trend will continue to grow).[138] That means more and more companies research your social media profiles to evaluate your character and personality. What they find about you will influence their hiring decision.

To help you better appreciate the role of social media in your job search, CareerBuilder.com conducted a survey that asked more than 2,100 hiring managers and human resource professionals if, how, and why they incorporate social media into their hiring process.

In the CareerBuilder survey, employers who chose not to pursue a job applicant after researching social media sites indicated the following reasons:

- Job seeker posted inappropriate pictures—46 percent
- Found evidence of job seeker's use of alcohol or drugs—40 percent
- Job seeker made negative remarks about previous employer—34 percent

---

138 Rossheim, John. "Social Networking: The Art of Social Media Recruiting," Monster, February 11, 2015, http://hiring.monster.com/hr/hr-best-practices/recruiting-hiring-advice/job-screening- techniques/recruiting-using-social-media.aspx (accessed August 26, 2015).

- Inappropriate comments made about race, gender, religion, and so on—29 percent[139]

However, over 30 percent of hiring executives discovered information that improved a job seeker's candidacy, including:

- Job seeker's background matched qualifications of position—42 percent
- Got a good feel for candidate's personality—38 percent
- Professionalism—38 percent
- Creativity—36 percent
- Communication—37 percent[140]

According to CareerBuilder, the research clearly indicates that employers (and your networking contacts) will utilize social media to gain additional insight into job seekers' behavior and personality. Which means you should be certain your social media profiles are as effective in networking and your job search as they can be.

---

139 CareerBuilder, "35 Percent of Employers Less Likely to Interview Applicants They Can't Find Online, According to Annual CareerBuilder Social Media Recruitment Survey," news release, May 14, 2015, http://www.careerbuilder.com/share/aboutus/pressreleasesdetail.aspx?sd=5%2F14%2F2015&id=pr893&ed=12%2F31%2F2015 (accessed June 1, 2015).

140 Ibid.

Appendix

Success Story Worksheet and Samples

Employer:

Your Position:

When:

Skill/Competency:

Challenge (Situation/Task):

Action:

Result:

Success Story—Example #1

Employer: XYZ Insurance Company

Position: Vice President of Product Development and Contracting

When: 20XX

Skill/Competency: Creativity, Critical Thinking, and Analysis

Challenge: While I was working at a large national insurance carrier [you would use the actual name in your story], their workers' compensation product portfolio was missing an ancillary product line/division. This was causing us to miss out on a potential revenue stream and the opportunity to compete against those companies providing these products as a standalone service.

The theory was that by adding ancillary services we would add revenue, increase customer retention, and promote long-term loyalty from our existing client base.

Action: We developed a new line of contracts for ancillary providers. We established a list of providers in multiple fields, i.e., DME,[141] O and P, home health, and so on. With these providers, we contracted and negotiated pricing. Once we had 80 percent of the contracts signed, we began marketing the new product offerings through conferences, seminars, and email blasts to existing and potential clients. At the same time, we developed a fully insured product that provided us with a one-stop-shop ability to service existing and potential clients.

Result: The end result of this effort was our ability to grow the bottom-line revenue by 27 percent in the first year after the network was up and running. This product division stands today and continues to grow.

---

141 "Durable medical equipment"; see "Durable Medical Equipment (DME) Center," Centers for Medicare & Medicaid Services, http://www.cms.gov/Center/Provider-Type/Durable-Medical-Equipment-DME-Center.html (accessed July 13, 2015).

Success Story—Example #2

Employer: ABC Company

Position: COO/Legal Counsel

When: 20XX

Skill/Competency: Communication, Presentation, Relationship/ Trust Building

Challenge: With hundreds of legal actions pending against the company because of a product that admittedly enticed litigious behavior, our task was to alleviate current and prospective clients' anxieties.

Action: Focus client attention on the product's results, not on what could or might happen. There were more than one hundred filings against the company, but less than 5 percent resulted in a hearing, and more than half of those settled prior to the actual hearing date. When there was a hearing, only a handful resulted in the client paying full bill charges.

Result: As a result, when netting the entire portfolio of a client's book of bills, the company would save 40 percent or more off the allowable charges. Once the message changed from trying to minimize the risk, to acknowledging the risk and then aggregating the impact of the entire book of bills, clients were able to put it in perspective. The odds of a lawsuit that resulted in a hearing and the client having to pay full bill charges were similar to driving a car and anticipating an accident. Tens of thousands of people drive cars each day and arrive safely to their destination. Furthermore, we chose to indemnify clients for any expenses so that their greatest risk would be to pay total bill charges, which was what they were asked to pay in the first place. As a result, clients not only stayed with the company, but we were able to add numerous high-profile clients. The net growth of the business was seven times initial revenues with incredibly generous margins in excess of any industry standard.

Success Story—Example #3

Employer: National Company

Position: Senior Vice President of Sales

When: 20XX

Skill/Competency: Creativity, Analytical Thinking, and Problem Solving

Challenge: The firm had experienced four years of flat or declining revenues. As a result, the owner despised salespeople, as he was not seeing a return on investment. He refused to spend the requisite resources to secure the talent needed to compete in the marketplace. I was brought in to reverse the revenue trend and add more staff at a lower-than-competitive market rate of compensation.

Action: Not having resources to secure the talent to compete on an individual basis, and not having a corporate reputation to help recruit talent, I chose a slightly different strategy. I convinced the owner that I was going to secure top-tier talent using cumulative budget dollars. In essence, I hired two people with the money that had been allocated for three new hires.

Additionally, I had to focus existing resources on the market segments where they could win business. The high-powered talent was directed to large national opportunities, and the existing talent was redirected to regional opportunities. I helped both national and regional colleagues target and secure value-added resellers. The resellers created a one-to-many relationship, and once we worked out the economics, these resellers approached clients they already had and created a revenue stream for them and us.

Result: The result was a 14 percent growth rate for the business by the end of year one. We were able to capture some very competent sales talent as the reps began to earn healthy commissions compared to other regional and national colleagues selling the same services.

Networking Follow-Up Letter

Date
Mr. John Baker
President
BFO Company
1200 Market Boulevard
Whitewater, Michigan 19117

RE: Our lunch on Tuesday

Dear Mr. Baker,

Thank you for meeting me for lunch Tuesday. It was a pleasure getting together with a fellow Lambda Chi alumnus. When I came across your name in the alumni directory, I never realized we would have so much in common. It was such a coincidence that you know Brian Klein and Mike Allen, my "brothers" from the University of Nebraska. What a small world!

As we discussed, the plastics industry has changed so dramatically over the last five years. It is such an exciting time. I know I have the skills and experience needed to help a company make the changes necessary to become a player in today's marketplace. As I pointed out, some of my most recent accomplishments have been:

• Assisted plant manager with implementation of comprehensive safety program, which resulted in zero time-loss accidents in 20XX.

• Led engineering team to overhaul manufacturing process, which increased production by 40 percent.

• Reengineered department to increase efficiencies and cut labor costs by $100,000 per year, while maintaining productivity.

I appreciate your advice, and the contacts you supplied me with. I will be contacting those individuals this week. In the meantime, please feel free to call me at (123) 555-4567 if you hear of any opportunities that may fit my background.

John, if there is anything I can do to return the favor, please just pick up the phone. Thanks again!

Sincerely,
Dustin Jasien

Introductory Email to a Search Firm

Subject Line: #1 Work Comp Services Sales Professional

Mr. Johnson,

I am a top-producing Workers' Compensation Services Sales Professional who ranked as the number one sales representative amongst my peers for 20XX and 20XX. I played an instrumental role in the growth of my former employer.

My sales achievements include:

1. Consistently exceeded sales quotas for the last four years.

2. Ranked number one in sales in 20XX and 20XX. Sales Representative of the Year.

3. 20XX—Account Coordinator of the Year Award.

Click here to watch a brief one-minute bio video.

I sold pharmacy services, transportation, translation, home health, physical therapy, durable medical equipment, and other services within the workers' compensation and auto insurance industries. Territory includes the Great Lakes area calling on nurse case managers, claims managers, and adjusters, among others. I have no restrictions on travel.

If there is a possible fit with one of your clients, I would like to speak with you about that opportunity. In the alternative, if I am a candidate who fits your specialty, please keep me in mind for future opportunities.

I have attached a resume for review.

Best Regards,
Your Name
Contact Information

Bibliography

Adams, Susan. "4 Ways to Use Twitter to Find a Job." Forbes. November 30, 2012. http://www.forbes.com/sites/susanadams/2012/11/30/4-ways-to-use-twitter-to-find-a-job/ (accessed June 16, 2015).

Andrew, Victoria. "The Power of a Positive Attitude." Blog. Kavaliro Employment Agency. May 23, 2013. http://www.kavaliro.com/the-power-of-a-positive-attitude (accessed June 8, 2015).

Arruda, William. "Is LinkedIn Poised To Be The Next Media Giant?" *Forbes*. March 8, 2015. http://www.forbes.com/sites/williamarruda/2015/03/08/is-linkedin-poised-to-be-the-next-media-giant/ (accessed June 5, 2015).

Asher, Donald. *Cracking the Hidden Job Market: How to Find Opportunity in Any Economy*. New York: Ten Speed Press, 2011.

Ayele, Daniel. "Land Your Dream Job in 2015 with These Data-Proven LinkedIn Tips." LinkedIn Blog. January 29, 2015. http://blog.linkedin.com/2015/01/29/jobseeking-tips/ (accessed June 9, 2015).

Ayres, Leslie. "Why You Need a Resume Business Card." *The Job Search Guru* (blog). March 16, 2009. http://www.thejobsearchguru.com/notesfrom/why-you-need-a-resume-business-card/ (accessed November 4, 2015).

Bergdahl, Michael. *What I Learned From Sam Walton: How to Compete and Thrive in a Wal-Mart World*. Hoboken, New Jersey: John Wiley & Sons, 2004.

BusinessDictionary.com. "Networking." http://www.businessdictionary.com/definition/networking.html (accessed November 12, 2015).

Byrne, Donn Erwin. *The Attraction Paradigm*. New York: Academic Press, 1971. CareerBuilder. "Get Help With Hiring . . . And More: Working With Staffing Firms: What's in It for Me?" http://www.careerbuildercommunications.com/staffing-firms/ (accessed June 19, 2015).

CareerBuilder. "35 Percent of Employers Less Likely to Interview Applicants They Can't Find Online, According to Annual CareerBuilder Social Media Recruitment Survey." News release. May 14, 2015. http://www.careerbuilder.com/share/aboutus/pressreleasesdetail.aspx?sd=5%2F14%2F2015&id=pr893&ed=12%2F31%2F2015 (accessed June 1, 2015).

Centers for Medicare & Medicaid Services. "Durable Medical Equipment (DME) Center." http://www.cms.gov/Center/Provider-Type/Durable-Medical-Equipment-DME-Center.html (accessed July 13, 2015).

Cialdini, Robert B. *Influence: Science and Practice.* Fourth edition. Needham Heights, MA: Allyn & Bacon, 2001.

Claycomb, Heather, and Karl Dinse. *Career Pathways—Interactive Workbook.* (1995).

Coburn, Derek. *Networking Is Not Working: Stop Collecting Business Cards and Start Making Meaningful Connections.* IdeaPress Publishing, 2014.

Cockburn, Sue. "Create Your Custom LinkedIn Web Address in 5 Easy Steps." *Growing Social Biz* (blog). September 30, 2015. http://growingsocialbiz.com/simple-steps-creating-your-customized-linkedin-url/ (accessed November 12, 2015).

Collamer, Nancy. "The Perfect Elevator Pitch to Land a Job." *Forbes.* February 4, 2013. http://www.forbes.com/sites/nextavenue/2013/02/04/the-perfect-elevator-pitch-to-land-a-job/ (accessed May 28, 2015).

Cuddy, Amy. "Your Body Language Shapes Who You Are." TEDGlobal video, 21:02. Filmed June 2012. http://www.ted.com/talks/amy_cuddy_your_body_language_shapes_who_you_are?language=en (accessed March 17, 2016).

Design Aglow (blog). "10 Ways You're Building a Fantastic Brand." February 3, 2015. http://designaglow.com/blogs/design-aglow/16728432-10-ways-youre-building-a-fantastic-brand (accessed May 28, 2015).

Dickler, Jessica. "Get Your Holiday Job—on Twitter!" CNNMoney. October 21, 2010. http://money.cnn.com/2010/10/21/pf/job_openings_on_twitter/ (accessed June 4, 2015).

DiResta, Diane. Interview by Christina Canters. "Episode 29—How to Blitz

Your Job Interview—Secrets of Executive Speech Coach Diane Diresta."
DesignDrawSpeak. Podcast audio. June 12, 2014. http://designdrawspeak.
com/029/ (accessed June 19, 2015).

DISYS. "Top 5 Reasons to Use Staffing Firms as Your Primary Hiring
Strategy."   http://www.disys.com/top-5-reasons-to-use-staffing-firms-as-
your-primary-hiring-strategy/ (accessed June
19, 2015).

Dougherty, Lisa. "16 Tips to Optimize Your LinkedIn Profile and Your
Personal Brand." LinkedIn Pulse. July 8, 2014. https://www.linkedin.com/
pulse/20140708162049-7239647-16-tips-to-optimize-your-linkedin-profile-
and-enhance-your-personal-brand (accessed November 11, 2015).

Duggan, Maeve, Nicole B. Ellison, Cliff Lampe, Amanda Lenhart, and
Mary Madden. "Demographics of Key Social Networking Platforms."
Pew Research Center. January 9, 2015. http://www.pewinternet.org/
2015/01/09/demographics-of-key-social-networking-platforms-2/
(accessed June 16, 2015).

Frasco, Stephanie. "11 Tips to Help Optimize Your LinkedIn Profile for
Maximum Exposure and Engagement." Convert with Content (blog).
https://www.convertwithcontent.com/11-tips-optimize-linkedin-profile-
maximum-exposure-engagement/ (accessed June 10, 2015).

Geoff. "Top LinkedIn Facts and Stats [Infographic]." We Are Social Media
(blog). July 25, 2014. http://wersm.com/top-linkedin-facts-and-stats-
infographic/ (accessed May 29, 2015).

Go Lean Six Sigma. "What is Lean Six Sigma?" https://goleansixsigma.
com/what-is-lean-six-sigma/ (accessed July 8, 2015).

Goodreads. "David Ogilvy Quotable Quote." http://www.goodreads.com/
quotes/262108-jodon-t-bunt-aim-out-of-the-ballpark-aim-for-the (accessed
May 28, 2015).

Goodreads. "Jarod Kintz Quotable Quote." http://www.goodreads.com/
quotes/1234580-the-only-people-who-don-t-need-elevator-pitches-are-
elevator (accessed May 28, 2015).

Goodreads. "Johann Wolfgang von Goethe Quotable Quote." http://www.
goodreads.com/quotes/316359-just-begin-and-the-mind-grows-heated-
continue-and-the (accessed June 11, 2015).

Goodreads. "Ralph Waldo Emerson Quotable Quote." www.goodreads. com/quotes/60285-do-the-thing-you-fear-and-the-death-of-fear (accessed May 28, 2015).

Graham, Brian. *Get Hired Fast! Tap the Hidden Job Market in 15 Days*. Avon, MA: Adams Media, 2005.

Hallowell, Kirk. *The Million Dollar Race: An Insider's Guide to Winning Your Dream Job*. Austin, TX: Greenleaf Book Group Press, 2013.

Hansen, Randall S., PhD. "Networking Business Cards: An Essential Job-Search Tool for Job-Seekers, Career Changers, and College Students When a Resume Just Won't Do." *Quintessential Careers*. http://www.quintcareers. com/networking-business-cards/ (accessed November 4, 2015).

Hansen, Randall S., PhD, and Katharine Hansen, PhD. "What Do Employers *Really* Want? Top Skills and Values Employers Seek from Job-Seekers." *Quintessential Careers*. http://www.quintcareers.com/job_skills_values. html (accessed May 27, 2015).

Hanson, Arik. "Should You Put MBA Behind Your Name on Your LinkedIn Profile?" LinkedIn Pulse. May 29, 2014. https://www.linkedin.com/ pulse/20140529131058-18098999-should-you-put-mba-behind-your-name-on-your-linkedin-profile (accessed July 17, 2015).

HelpGuide.org. "Job Networking Tips." http://www.helpguide.org/ articles/work-career/job-networking-tips.htm (accessed November 3, 2015).

IBISWorld. "Employment and Recruiting Agencies in the US: Market Research Report." March 2015. http://www.ibisworld.com/ industry/default.aspx?indid=1463 (accessed June 11, 2015).

International Foundation of Employee Benefit Plans, Inc. "About the CEBS Program." https://www.ifebp.org/CEBSDesignation/overview/Pages/ default.aspx (accessed November 12, 2015).

Isaacson, Nate. "Professional Designations Are Great But They Are Not a Part of Your Name." LinkedIn Pulse. April 14, 2014. https://www.linkedin. com/pulse/20140414223601-23236063-professional-designations-are-great-but-they-are-not-a-part-of-your-name (accessed July 16, 2015).

Jamal, Nina, and Judith Lindenberger. "How to Make a Great First Impression." Business Know-How. http://www.businessknowhow.com/growth/dress-impression.htm (accessed June 2, 2015).

Jobvite. "Jobvite Social Recruiting Survey Finds Over 90% of Employers Will Use Social Recruiting in 2012." News release. July 9, 2012. http://www.jobvite.com/press-releases/2012/jobvite-social-recruiting-survey-finds-90-employers-will-use-social-recruiting-2012/ (accessed November 10, 2015).

Jobvite. "2014 Social Recruiting Survey." https://www.jobvite.com/wp-content/June 1, 2015).

Knyszweski, Jerome. "How to Use LinkedIn as a Student—And Nail That Dream Job." LinkedIn Pulse. April 28, 2015. https://www.linkedin.com/pulse/how-use-linkedin-student-nail-dream-job-jerome-knyszewski (accessed May 28, 2015).

Konnikova, Maria. "The Limits of Friendship." The New Yorker. October 7, 2014. http://www.newyorker.com/science/maria-konnikova/social-media-affect-math-dunbar-number-friendships (accessed November 10, 2015).

Kurtzberg, Terri R., and Charles E. Naquin. The Essentials of Job Negotiations: Proven Strategies for Getting What You Want. Santa Barbara, CA: Praeger, 2011.

Leadership Now. "Quotes on Initiative." http://www.leadershipnow.com/initiativequotes.html (accessed May 28, 2015).

Leanne, Shelly. How to Interview Like a Top MBA: Job-Winning Strategies from Headhunters, Fortune 100 Recruiters, and Career Counselors. New York: McGraw-Hill, 2004.

Leibman, Pete. "9 Keys on How to Email a New Networking Contact During a Job Search." CareerMuscles (blog). January 6, 2011. https://careermuscles.wordpress.com/2011/01/06/9-keys-on-how-to-email-a-new-networking-contact-during-a-job-search-written-by-career-expert-pete-leibman/ (accessed November 10, 2015).

LinkedIn. "Profile Completeness." https://www.linkedin.com/static?key=pop%2Fpop_more_profile_completeness (accessed May 29, 2015)

LinkedIn. "Using LinkedIn to Find a Job or Internship." https://university.linkedin.com/content/dam/university/global/en_US/site/pdf/TipSheet_FindingaJoborInternship.pdf (accessed June 7, 2015).

LinkedIn Help Center. "InMail—Overview." https://help.linkedin.com/app/answers/detail/a_id/1584/~/InMail---overview (accessed June 24, 2015).

LinkedIn Help Center. "Showing or Hiding Activity Updates About You." https://help.linkedin.com/app/answers/detail/a_id/78/~/showing-or-hiding-activity-updates-about-you (accessed June 2, 2015).

LinkedIn Newsroom. "About LinkedIn." https://press.linkedin.com/about-linkedin (accessed May 29, 2015).

LinkedIn Talent Solutions. "2015 Talent Trends: Insights for Research and Staffing Recruiters on What Talent Wants Around the World." https://business.linkedin.com/content/dam/business/talent-solutions/global/en_us/c/pdfs/global-talent-trends-staff-report.pdf (accessed July 17, 2015).

LinkHumans. "10 Tips for the Perfect LinkedIn Profile." Slideshare. Published July 1, 2014. http://www.slideshare.net/linkedin/10-tips-for-the-perfect-linkedin-profile (accessed November 11, 2015).

LLM Guide. "What Is an LLM?" http://www.llm-guide.com/what-is-an-llm (accessed November 10, 2015).

Moynihan, Lisa M., Mark V. Roehling, Marcie A. LePine, and Wendy R. Boswell. "A Longitudinal Study of the Relationships Among Job Search Self-Efficacy, Job Interviews, and Employment Outcomes." Abstract. Journal of Business and Psychology 18, no. 2 (2003): 201–233. http://link.springer.com/article/10.1023%2FA%3A1027349115277#/page-1 (accessed July 3, 2015).

Nsehe, Mfonobong. "19 Inspirational Quotes From Nelson Mandela." Forbes.com. December 6, 2013. http://www.forbes.com/sites/mfonobongnsehe/2013/12/06/20-inspirational-quotes-from-nelson-mandela/ (accessed May 27, 2015).

Oswal, Shreya. "7 Smart Habits of Successful Job Seekers [INFOGRAPHIC]." LinkedIn Blog. March 19, 2014. http://blog.linkedin.com/2014/03/19/7-smart-habits-of-successful-job-seekers-infographic/ (accessed June 9, 2015).

Phillips, Simon. The Complete Guide to Professional Networking:The Secrets of Online and Offline Success. London: Kogan Page Limited, 2014.

Pine, Joslyn. Editor. Book of African-American Quotations. New York: Dover Publications, 2011.

Pollak, Lindsey. "How to Attract Employers' Attention on LinkedIn." LinkedIn Blog. December 2, 2010. http://blog.linkedin.com/2010/12/02/find-jobs-on-linkedin/ (accessed June 4, 2015).

Popik, Barry. "It's not what you know, but who you know." The Big Apple. October 9, 2009. http://www.barrypopik.com/index.php/new_york_city/entry/its_not_what_you_know_but_who_you_know/ (accessed November 10, 2015).

Recovery Ranch, The. "Doing What's Necessary, What's Possible, and What Seems to be Impossible." http://www.recoveryranch.com/articles/necessary-possible-impossible/ (accessed May 27, 2015).

Regis University Career Services. "Interviewing Strategies for CPS Students and Alumni." http://www.regis.edu/About-Regis-University/University-Offices-and-Services/Career-Services/Student-and-Alumni/Interviewing-Strategies.aspx (accessed June 19, 2015).

Reynolds, Marci. "How to Be Found More Easily in LinkedIn (LinkedIn SEO)." Job-Hunt.org. http://www.job-hunt.org/social-networking/be-found-on-linkedin.shtml (accessed June 4, 2015).

Rossheim, John. "Social Networking: The Art of Social Media Recruiting." Monster. February 11, 2015. http://hiring.monster.com/hr/hr-best-practices/recruiting-hiring-advice/job-screening-techniques/recruiting-using-social-media.aspx (accessed August 26, 2015).

Rothberg, Steven. "80% of Job Openings are Unadvertised." College Recruiter (blog). March 28, 2013. https://www.collegerecruiter.com/blog/2013/03/28/80-of-job-openings-are-unadvertised/ (accessed June 11, 2015).

Sachdeva, Gyanda. "Unlocking Your Competitive Edge with the Power of LinkedIn Premium." LinkedIn Blog. December 18, 2014. http://blog.linkedin.com/2014/12/18/unlocking-your-competitive-edge-with-the-power-of-linkedin-premium/ (accessed June 9, 2015).

Safani, Barbara. "Tell a Story Interviewers Can't Forget." TheLadders. http://www.theladders.com/career-advice/tell-story-interviewers-cant-forget (accessed May 29, 2015).

Serdula, Donna. "LinkedIn's New Requirements for a 100% Complete Profile." LinkedIn Makeover (blog). February 20, 2012. http://www.linkedin-makeover.com/2012/02/20/linkedins-new-requirements-for-a-100-complete-profile/ (accessed November 5, 2015).

Smith, Craig. "By the Numbers: 125+ Amazing LinkedIn Statistics." Last updated November 4, 2015. http://expandedramblings.com/index.php/by-the-numbers-a-few-important-linkedin-stats/ (accessed November 11, 2015).

Smith, Jacquelyn. "Here's What To Say In Your LinkedIn 'Summary' Statement." Business Insider. December 19, 2014. http://www.businessinsider.com/what-to-say-in-your-linkedin-summary-statement-2014-12 (accessed July 9, 2015).

Smith, Jacquelyn. "The Complete Guide to Crafting a Perfect LinkedIn Profile." Business Insider. January 21, 2015. http://www.businessinsider.com/guide-to-perfect-linkedin-profile-2015-1 (accessed June 4, 2015).

Tilus, Grant. "Top 10 Human Resources Job Skills Employers Want to See." Blog. Rasmussen College. July 29, 2013. http://www.rasmussen.edu/degrees/business/blog/human-resources-job-skills-employers-want-to-see/ (accessed July 10, 2015).

Townsend, Maya. "The Introvert's Survival Guide to Networking." Inc.com. http://www.inc.com/maya-townsend/introvert-networking-guide.html (accessed November 4, 2015).

True Source (blog). "Don't Do That!—Mistakes To Avoid When Working With Recruiters." November 2012. http://www.true-source.com/2012/11/dont-do-that-mistakes-to-avoid-when-working-with-recruiters/ (accessed June 9, 2015).

United States Army. "Operational Unit Diagrams." http://www.army.mil/info/organization/unitsandcommands/oud/ (accessed November 10, 2015).
U.S. Constitution Online. "Constitutional Topic: The Cabinet." http://www.usconstitution.net/consttop_cabi.html (accessed November 10, 2015).

US Department of Labor. "Frequently Asked Questions About Retirement Plans and ERISA." http://www.dol.gov/ebsa/faqs/faq_consumer_pension.html (accessed July 8, 2015).

Vaughan, Pamela. "81% of LinkedIn Users Belong to a LinkedIn Group [Data]." Hubspot Blogs. August 11, 2011. http://blog.hubspot.com/blog/tabid/6307/bid/22364/81-of-LinkedIn-Users-Belong-to-a-LinkedIn-Group-Data.aspx (accessed June 8, 2015).

Vlooten, Dick van. "The Seven Laws of Networking: Those Who Give, Get." Career Magazine. May 7, 2004. http://sciencecareers.sciencemag.org/career_magazine/previous_issues/articles/2004_05_07/nodoi.1275810282259244595 (accessed June 16, 2015).

Walters, Lillet. Secrets of Successful Speakers: How You Can Motivate, Captivate, and Persuade. New York: McGraw-Hill, 1993.

Weiss, Tara. "Find Your Job by Going to a Conference." Forbes. March 24, 2009. http://www.forbes.com/2009/03/24/conference-job-seeking-leadership-careers-networking.html (accessed July 10, 2015).

Whitcomb, Susan Britton. Job Search Magic: Insider Secrets from America's Career and Life Coach. Indianapolis, IN: JIST Works, 2006.

Williams, Armstrong. "A Few Simple Steps to Building Wealth." Townhall. June 13, 2005. http://townhall.com/columnists/armstrongwilliams/2005/06/13/a_few_simple_steps_to_building_wealth/page/full (accessed May 28, 2015).

Yate, Martin John. Knock 'em Dead Social Networking for Job Search and Professional Success. Avon, MA: Adams Media, 2014.

Yate, Martin John. Knock 'em Dead—The Ultimate Job Search Guide. Avon, MA: Adams Media, 2014.

Zack, Devora. "10 Tips for People Who Hate Networking." Careerealism. May 4, 2015. http://www.careerealism.com/hate-networking-tips/ (accessed July 17, 2015).

Zolfagharifard, Ellie. "First Impressions Really DO Count: Employers Make Decisions About Job Applicants in Under Seven Minutes." Daily Mail. June 18, 2014. http://www.dailymail.co.uk/sciencetech/article-2661474/First-impressions-really-DO-count-Employers-make-decisions-job-applicants-seven-minutes.html (accessed June 5, 2015).